Early praise for *Program Management for Open Source Projects*

What I love about *Program Management for Open Source Projects* is how Ben's advice is clear and actionable. This is not theory, it is solid advice that open source program managers can use to effectively manage an open source project. Every open source program manager should read this book.

➤ **Jim Hall**
  Founder and Project Coordinator, The FreeDOS Project

A thorough exploration of program management, particularly as it relates to large scale open source projects. This book is both practical and informative, a great starting point for anyone wanting a better understanding of what program management entails.

➤ **Cate Huston**
  Engineering Manager, DuckDuckGo

I often wish we could just clone Ben. Since that technology seems far off, I'll do the next best thing: encourage you to read this book. The world needs more people who know what Ben shares here. It's full of experience-based wisdom about making an open source project work, with both specific examples and great insights into general concepts in the context of community-driven development. This book will be useful to anyone in an open source leadership role — or anyone interested in helping a community they care about.

➤ **Matthew Miller**
  Fedora Project Leader and Distinguished Engineer, Red Hat

In open source as in life, there are no "unskilled jobs" and worthy outcomes do not "just happen." I've seen too many open source projects and communities ruined by these misconceptions. Now, with this book, Ben has given us the resources needed to help more projects be successful. This book brilliantly disproves the perception that managing a successful open source project is easy, while effectively and empathetically providing the lessons for doing it well. This is exactly the resource I've needed for helping companies understand what's involved in managing an open source project well.

➤ **VM (Vicky) Brasseur**
   Open Source Business Strategist, self

Program Management for Open Source Projects

How to Guide Your Community-Driven, Open Source Project

Ben Cotton

The Pragmatic Bookshelf

Raleigh, North Carolina

Many of the designations used by manufacturers and sellers to distinguish their products are claimed as trademarks. Where those designations appear in this book, and The Pragmatic Programmers, LLC was aware of a trademark claim, the designations have been printed in initial capital letters or in all capitals. The Pragmatic Starter Kit, The Pragmatic Programmer, Pragmatic Programming, Pragmatic Bookshelf, PragProg and the linking *g* device are trademarks of The Pragmatic Programmers, LLC.

Every precaution was taken in the preparation of this book. However, the publisher assumes no responsibility for errors or omissions, or for damages that may result from the use of information (including program listings) contained herein.

For our complete catalog of hands-on, practical, and Pragmatic content for software developers, please visit *https://pragprog.com*.

The team that produced this book includes:

CEO: Dave Rankin
COO: Janet Furlow
Managing Editor: Tammy Coron
Development Editor: Michael Swaine
Copy Editor: Corina Lebegioara
Indexing: Potomac Indexing, LLC
Layout: Gilson Graphics
Founders: Andy Hunt and Dave Thomas

For sales, volume licensing, and support, please contact *support@pragprog.com*.

For international rights, please contact *rights@pragprog.com*.

ISBN-13: 978-1-68050-924-3
Book version: P1.0—July 2022

Contents

Acknowledgments

Thank you to my development editor, Michael Swaine. Mike's expert guidance and support turned my thoughts into a polished book. The rest of the team at The Pragmatic Bookshelf has been wonderful as well. This book could not exist without their hard work.

To Eleanor, Bryan, and Miranda, thank you for your love and support. You had to hear "not right now, I'm writing" far more than I'd have liked, but I couldn't have done this without you. And to all of my other friends and family, your support and encouragement kept me going.

Thank you to my technical reviewers: Robyn Bergeron, VM Brasseur, Jim Hall, Cate Huston, Jen Krieger, Luboš Kocman, Deb Nicholson, John Poelstra, and Jaroslav Reznik. I'm still flattered that people who I admire and respect so much would take the time to help me with this project.

For all of the editors that I've worked with over the years, thanks for helping me become a better writer. And thank you to Matt Simmons for making me think that there are people out there who want to read what I write in the first place.

There are two things that authors fear most: 1. that nobody will buy their book; 2. that people will read it. So thank you to all of the beta readers who made fear number two come true. I appreciate your willingness to take a risk on an unfinished book and greatly appreciate the feedback.

Last, but certainly not least, I owe so much to the coworkers and open source communities that I've learned from over the years. To thank everyone by name would double the size of this book, but I do want to specifically call out my Fedora Program Manager predecessors: John, Robyn, Jaroslav, and Jan. They're the giants on whose shoulders I stand. So much of what I share in this book comes from the lessons I learned from them. Thanks, too, to the communities that I'm not a part of but that I've watched from afar to gain other perspectives. When we work in the open, everyone benefits.

Everyone does program management, some just do it poorly.
> Ben Cotton

Introduction

This epigraph from Ben Cotton isn't simply a fun, self-congratulating laugh line I use in presentations. It represents a fundamental truth of complex technical undertakings: you can't avoid program management, so you might as well do it deliberately. Whether or not you realize it, you're already *doing* the work of program management. This book gives you the tools to do the work consciously and do it well.

What a Program Manager Does

As a program manager, you coordinate the efforts of the contributor community to meet the project's goals. The title "Chief Cat-Herding Officer" is a joke, but an apt one. You're working with a group largely or entirely composed of volunteers to produce software that other people will want to use. Individually, contributors have their own interests and goals. When you're a successful program manager, you get these individuals aligned in the same general direction to meet the overall goals of the community.

If you've seen the movie *Finding Nemo*, you may have a visual in mind (except with fish, not cats). Nemo is a fish separated from his father. In one scene, he's swimming with a school of tuna that gets scooped up in a fishing net. The tuna are swimming every which way as the net slowly hauls them in. But Nemo gets them all to swim downward. Once they're all working in the same direction, the fishing boat's motor can't haul the net in. The rope breaks and the fish all escape the net. This is what you're doing, except with lower stakes.

Some open source projects have a role explicitly named "program manager." Others have a "release manager" or similar title. Most projects have neither, but someone is still doing the work. It could be the project leader, a member of the technical steering committee, or an organized and enthusiastic contributor with no particular role. Wherever you are in the project's structure (or lack thereof), you're keeping everyone informed and helping folks find the information and resources they need.

This book covers all aspects of program management, from scheduling to feature management, bug tracking, and beyond. You might find as you read this book that you're sharing some of these duties with other members of the project. That's okay. The important part is that *someone* in your project is consciously working on each aspect. If you're not thinking about the work, that doesn't mean it's not happening. It means it's probably not happening well.

Why Program Management Is Important

Open source projects produce software, but they're run by people. People are dynamic and sometimes unpredictable. The more people are involved, the more unpredictable the project becomes. As a program manager, you bring order to the chaos. You don't do this by imposing order from the top down—that's not how open source projects work. Instead, you *give structure to the agreements of the community.*

When you're doing your job well, it can appear effortless. But I suspect that most projects that thrive in the long term aren't successful by accident. They don't keep everything working smoothly without effort. Instead, someone (or several people) does the work to coordinate effort across the project. And that can get complicated quickly. The number of communication channels in a team goes up exponentially as the team grows.[1] Communication overhead gets even heavier in open source projects where members of the team come and go, sometimes without warning. A successful program manager reduces the overhead by collecting and distributing information across the project.

In addition, an experienced program manager is an expert on processes. Some open source developers may think their project doesn't need any processes. But a process is simply the way you do things. You always have processes. The only question is whether the processes are predictable and serve the needs of the project or they're ad hoc and subject to the whims of whoever is doing work at the moment. Process development is a skill like software testing or documentation writing. But again, you can't impose it from above. As the program manager, you work as a consultant to the rest of the project, helping everyone come up with processes that best meet their needs.

Open source projects, like all human systems, are naturally chaotic. Deliberate program management gives the community, users, and sponsors reliable and predictable insight into the current state of the project and the trends that

---

1.   https://hbr.org/2009/05/why-teams-dont-work

hint at the future. It's much easier to do something well when you're doing it on purpose.

Why You Want This Book

Hopefully, you now have a clear picture of what program management is and why it's important to your project. This book will help you put this knowledge into action. Think of it as a do-it-yourself kit, except the instructions are clearly written and you don't have any Allen wrenches to keep track of. You'll come away from it with the tools and perspective you need to build the right processes for your project.

Your journey will start with a look at the basic principles of program management. Next, we'll briefly cover project management to help you understand the similarities and differences. Then you'll learn about a few fundamental skills that will touch all aspects of your program management work: relationships, decision-making, and meetings. From there, you'll learn about what's necessary to take a release from start to finish. You'll learn how to develop a schedule, plan features, track bugs, and more.

You'll see how you can apply the discipline of program management to your own open source project. You'll be guided to think about how the lessons in this book apply to your project. You'll see examples of what has worked well—and I'll also share some of my mistakes.

No matter how large or small your project is, you will be able to use what you learn in this book to be more intentional in managing your open source program.

## CHAPTER 1

Manage the Program

Program management is more than project management at scale. This chapter takes a look at what makes it different. The Project Management Institute defines[1] a program as "a group of related projects managed in a coordinated manner to obtain benefits not available from managing them individually." The word "benefit" is key here: projects result in deliverables, while programs result in benefits. So projects are the "how" you deliver the "why" of a program. Programs don't have a defined end. They continue until the benefit they deliver is no longer required. Your open source project? It's actually a program (more on that in the next chapter).

Take the Big Picture View

Problem: You get bogged down in the details and lose sight of what's going on in the rest of the community.

To know what's going on, you have to look at the big picture. Don't look at the trees when there's a whole forest to see. When you're an effective program manager, the details rarely matter.

At first glance, you might think that program management is like project management, but on a larger scale. You're not wrong, but that's not fully right. Many of the skills you use in managing projects apply to managing programs. I might even go as far as saying you can't be a good program manager unless you understand project management first. If you don't have a good grasp of project management, the next chapter will help you catch up.

On the other hand, mastering project management doesn't necessarily mean you're a great program manager. Project management is focused on the day-to-day activity of a team (or closely related teams). As a program manager,

---

1.   https://www.pmi.org/learning/featured-topics/program

you're more concerned about the *interfaces* between teams. You don't need to particularly care about *how* a team does their work so long as they deliver what other teams need from them on time. (As a program manager in an open source community, this is probably not entirely true for reasons you'll see later in this chapter.)

When you zoom out, you naturally decrease the resolution of what you see. Since management types like to talk in terms of airplane flight altitudes, let's use an aviation analogy. Being a program manager is like being the dispatcher for an airline. Your job is to make sure the planes get from one airport to another on schedule using an appropriate amount of fuel. You don't know or care who is sitting where on the plane or when the drinks are served. The flight crew, who are the project managers in this analogy, worry about that. So long as you don't end up with five planes all trying to get to the same gate at once, it doesn't matter to you how the flight crew runs their flight.

The zoomed-out view means you trade detail for context. As the program manager, you'll need to be aware of what's going on in all your community's teams. Similarly, you need to know what is happening in your upstream and downstream communities. Changes in schedules, shifts in how the technologies are implemented, or changes in the health of those communities will all have an impact on your own community. Watching your community's "market" and the technology sector at large will also help. Adjusting the code or the process can help you attract new contributors as the trends shift over time. And, of course, you can always learn lessons from what others have done well—or poorly.

Balance Priorities

Problem: Your community has limited time and resources, but it has limitless ideas for work to be done.

How do you correctly allocate limited resources across the community? You balance priorities. Balance doesn't mean fixing a static allocation forever. Similar to shifting your weight as you walk, balancing priorities is a dynamic activity.

Having a broader context, even beyond the scope of your community, is crucial to finding the balance. People will naturally focus on their own work. The deeper they work on something, the more their focus narrows. That's fine, but it can mean they lose the broader context. I'm sure you can think of a time when someone you were working with (or perhaps you) got so immersed in the details that they lost track of the "why" of the work. So what do you do when you have people deeply focused on two different areas that are competing for the same resource?

As the program manager, you're well-positioned to see the broader context. Your job isn't necessarily to make the decision. Instead, you can mediate the decision process in the broader community.

Be Aware of Your Own Overfocus

You're not immune from becoming too focused on something. The release schedule is a particularly attractive focal point. You want to get the release out on time, so you start to see everything through the "shipping the release on time" lens.

Just like the rest of your community, this isn't unexpected. But you need to watch out for this and try to pull yourself back to the broader context. Examine *why* an on-time release is important and ask yourself what you're trading off to stick to that goal.

As in a project, a program's time, cost, scope, and quality are considerations, but you have less control over them. The projects (in the context of your community, these are functional teams, special interest groups, and others) are semi-autonomous. Importantly, they receive their resources directly, not allocated from the program. So balancing the priorities is about balancing at the intersection of projects, not within projects. You're setting the boundaries that the projects operate within.

For example, imagine your infrastructure team wants to redeploy the testing infrastructure onto some shiny new hardware someone donated. Since space is limited, they have to take out the old hardware first. The QA team may say "that's fine, but we need to have it back online by the end of the month to test the release candidates." It doesn't matter to you how the infrastructure team does the work so long as it's done on time. And, in this case, delivery delays can probably be worked out between the infrastructure and QA teams. But then the company that had been hosting your chat servers goes out of business and the community decides that's not a risk they're willing to take again. Suddenly, your infrastructure team also needs to bring up new chat servers. What's more important to the community? Do you ask the infrastructure team to put the test infrastructure on hold and delay the release? Or do you find an alternative way to communicate in the short term? This is the program manager's balance.

I can't give you a magical formula for balancing priorities. How you rank your priorities is entirely context-dependent and shifts over time. Simplifying your install script may have been the most important issue at one point, but now you can hide the complexity by shipping a container. (That's an example. I personally think you should continue to simplify your install script because not everyone will want to run your app in a container, but I digress.)

It also depends on what you're trying to balance. The way you prioritize your own tasks will be different from prioritizing features in a release versus prioritizing work that goes into your infrastructure or community.

For tasks, the Eisenhower Matrix[2] is a simple approach. You classify every task as a pair of binary attributes: important or not important and urgent or not urgent. Start with the important and urgent tasks. Then move to the important and not urgent. These may be scheduled for the future. Next you tackle (or delegate) the urgent but not important tasks. Finally, if you have time, you do the not important and not urgent tasks. You may be surprised at how much time you save with this method because you're not sitting there trying to figure out which of a dozen tasks to do first.

When considering which features or bug fixes to put into a release, the MoSCoW[3] method provides a similar approach. Each feature is classified as "must have," "should have," "could have," or "won't have." Of course, the challenge here is two-fold: what if you have more must haves than time to do the work and how do you classify the features in the first place?

The answer to the first question is "take another pass, but this time with tighter standards for each level." Answering the second question could fill a book in itself, but here are a few principles to serve as a starting point.

- *Prefer finishing work.* If you have multiple-stage features, it's generally better to get one all the way done before starting on a new one. This gives your community a sense of accomplishment. Psychologically, it feels much better to have something *done*.

- *Prefer usability over capability.* This goes along with the previous item. If your software is hard to use, people will find something better. Having a good user experience will get people to stick around long enough for you to add missing features.

- *Prefer differentiation to catch-up.* Once you have the "table stakes" features, you should focus on the thing that makes your project special. Don't add features only because your competitors have them.

---

2.   https://www.eisenhower.me/eisenhower-matrix/
3.   https://en.wikipedia.org/wiki/MoSCoW_method

Take a similar approach when you're prioritizing infrastructure and community tasks. The MoSCoW method works well in this case, too; you simply need to think about an appropriate timebox for the planning. Here are a few principles to keep in mind as you work.

- *Prefer finishing work.* This is the same as in the previous list. Getting stuff done feels good and lets you get the full value of the effort.

- *Maximize the total benefit.* Think about benefits in two dimensions: the number of people who receive the benefit and the amount of benefit they receive. Something that saves 100 of your contributors an hour of effort a month is likely more important than something that saves 10 contributors three hours a month.

- *Reward the long-suffering.* Of course, if the same 10 people keep not getting the benefits, they'll get mad and go somewhere else. From time to time, you may want to jump something to the top of the stack as a way to reward particularly hard-working or patient contributors.

- *Expand the community.* Work that makes it easier for new users or contributors to join will have a huge payoff in the long run. Like the "prefer usability" point of the previous list, the idea is to get people into the community so they'll stick around to help with future work.

Prioritizing within the program is challenging work. Even when you have excellent guiding principles, it's not always easy to make decisions. You're dealing not only with objective facts but also with people's emotional attachment to their work or ideas. That's why mediating an agreement on prioritization works better in the long run than dictating a prioritization.

Your Turn

- Think about a time when the priorities were misbalanced on the work you were doing. How did this impact the program's ability to deliver the needed results?

- What unfinished tasks in your community can save a lot of contributors a little time? What tasks can save a few contributors a lot of time?

- Where do the tasks on your current to-do list fit into the Eisenhower Matrix? How do you personally decide what's urgent and what's important?

Manage Risks

Problem: You don't know what will send your program offtrack.

To understand the risks that can derail your program, you have to identify, track, and respond to them. In most cases, open source communities don't worry about risk at a fine level of detail. Perhaps this is because risk reflects uncertainty and with volunteer contributors, there's an inherent fuzziness to plans. Or maybe the lack of a revenue impact means that the community doesn't need to care as much. Whatever the reason, risk management tends to happen at a broader level. The risks are less about things that might delay the release for a week and more about the thing that might stop all progress.

Identify Risks

Problem: You don't know what events pose a risk to the program.

To start identifying risks, let's first define our terms. *Risk* is a reasonably foreseeable but uncertain event that could cause the project or program to fail to meet its objectives. Most definitions you'll find online include the word "uncertain," which means that the risk may or may not materialize, but "reasonably foreseeable" is just as important.

As a program manager, you want to be aware of and track the reasonable risks. What does that mean? Have you ever experienced an outage of your cloud provider? How about everyone being busy during a conference? Aliens invading and holding your project leader hostage? I hope we can agree that the last one isn't a reasonable risk. It's a waste of your time and focus to think about unreasonable risks. "Unreasonable" doesn't only mean "outlandish example used to make a point." Do you know how an exceptionally strong and well-aimed solar flare could severely damage the electronics on Earth? That's a plausible event, but if it happens, you'll have more important things to worry about. So file this in the "unreasonable" pile, too.

You've made a list of all of the things that could reasonably derail you. Next, you want to determine when it could manifest. For each risk, identify any *triggers*—events that cause the risk to materialize. The trigger isn't necessarily a single causal event; it can be the first outward sign that the risk is materializing.

Next, let's rank the risks by importance. How do we do that? Risk is two-dimensional, as we saw in the previous sunspot example. The first dimension is likelihood, often expressed as a probability (between 0—cannot happen—and 1—will definitely happen) or as a category (low, medium, or high likelihood).

Impact is the other dimension. For corporate programs, the impact may have a concrete value—dollar cost, additional effort required, reputation score, and so on. In open source projects, a categorical impact (high, medium, or low) is more useful. However you choose to score a risk, the most important are the high-impact, high-likelihood risks. The low-impact, low-likelihood risks are the least important. Somewhere in between are the rest. The specific ordering isn't particularly critical—you won't know which will actually appear until they do.

Track and Respond to Risks

Problem: There's no record of the risks you've identified. You don't know what to do if one of the risks materializes.

To make the work we did in the previous section helpful, you have to document the risks. Otherwise, who (including you!) will remember the details a month from now? A written record gives us something to work with as we do the next stage of risk management.

"But wait!" you say. "After I've identified and scored the risks, I'm not done?" Of course not! The point of identifying the risks is so that you can do something if they come to pass. This is your mitigation plan. Now that we have our risks recorded, our job is to track the risks. Be on the lookout for the risks' triggers (for example, a delay in the release of an upstream library that you depend on for new feature development). When the trigger occurs or appears imminent, it's time to put the mitigation strategy into play. Once a risk is no longer relevant (for example, the upstream release is out and works flawlessly), then you can stop tracking it.

Avoid Risks

Not all risk is bad. No risk, no reward, right? But as with bugs, it's cheaper to address risks earlier rather than later. If you have ways to minimize the impact before the risk materializes—or to avoid it entirely—then you should do that.

For example, you may design your project to use the current stable release of a library instead of the latest development release. This means you might miss out on some of the great new features, but it avoids the risk of the development release not being stable enough for production by the time you're ready to release your project. If you wait it out and you're wrong, you may have to deal with more bugs, back out some of your features, or have the library's API change in unexpected ways.

Mitigate Risks

In most cases, you'll end up addressing the impacts of a risk once it materializes. How exactly you do this will depend on the nature of the risk. If your build farm goes down, you might redeploy your infrastructure to a cloud provider. If a library you depend on releases late, you might delay your release or reengineer features that depend on it.

The point of mitigating a risk isn't to make it like the effect never happened. You're responding to it the best you can by minimizing the impact on the overall program. When deciding how you'll mitigate a risk, keep in mind your "business" requirements. Yes, open source projects have business requirements, even if you're not selling anything. Your release schedule, relationships with upstream and downstream projects, and the community's values are all important factors in determining the approach to take.

Accept Risks

Good news! Not every risk presents an existential threat. Sometimes you can simply ignore a risk. You know this intuitively, of course, but it's important to be conscious of it. Give yourself permission to ignore the low-impact risks, particularly if they're also low-probability.

When a risk's impact is lower than the cost of avoiding or mitigating it, the best thing you can do is nothing. For example, if the stickers you wanted to pass out at a conference were ordered too late, you could decide that it's not worth paying extra for a rush order. You can simply let them come late. There will be more conferences, after all.

Bringing Risk to the Fore

In my first few years as the Fedora Program Manager, I didn't give risk much conscious thought. Sure, we had risks to the release schedule, but they were generally things like "testing discovered a release-blocking bug that's hard to fix." These are the sorts of things you can reasonably expect, but given the number of packages that could cause such a bug, it's not practical to try to plan for all of them.

Then 2020 happened.

Our infrastructure team had already been planning a major datacenter move to happen shortly after the April release of Fedora Linux 32. As the COVID-19 pandemic began to take hold in the United States, a cross-country move became even dicier. Social distancing requirements limited the speed at which hardware in the old datacenter could be unracked. With stay-at-home orders and an increased demand for long-haul truckers, we had additional shipping delay risks.

Much of the hardware used for prerelease testing is located in Red Hat offices. Sudden office closures meant we couldn't get that test gear out, even if someone had the space to set it up at home. So we went into the beta and final releases with the state of our infrastructure and our ability to test the distribution at heightened risk.

Of course, there was also the risk that no one wanted to talk about. What happens if a key contributor got seriously ill—or worse? Who are the people that flip the right switches at the right time? How do we move forward with the release if they're not available?

Thankfully, everything turned out okay. One person did end up in the hospital for a bit, but they made a full recovery and we were able to cover their tasks without a hiccup. But it made me more aware of the ways that the program could be put at risk.

You don't have to plan for a global pandemic specifically, but it helps to know upon whose shoulders the world rests. Do what you can to share knowledge and responsibilities across people and geography. That way you're covered no matter what keeps someone from showing up.

Your Turn

- What risks have you encountered in your open source community? Where do they fit into the likelihood and impact matrix?

- When has anticipating a risk helped you with the impact when it materialized?

- How can you mitigate the risk to your community that you'll win the lottery and disappear to a private tropical island?

Report Status

Problem: Contributors don't know what important things are going on elsewhere in the community. They're disengaged and don't align their effort across teams.

Sometimes being a great program manager is less about doing and more about knowing and—more to the point—communicating what you know. Who did what? Which teams need help? How likely are we to meet our release target?

As a program manager, you're in an inherently cross-functional role. Because you're talking with all the parts of the community, you're in an ideal position to let everyone know what the others are doing.

In *The Mythical Man-Month [Bro95]*, Fred Brooks said "adding manpower to a late software project makes it later." His reasoning is simple: when more people are involved in a project, more communication channels are necessary because each person needs to communicate with all of the others. A key function of your job as the program manager is to counteract "Brooks' Law" by simplifying the communication channels.

Your job is to collect and report on the program's status—not only to the leaders or sponsors, although that's important too, but also to the community itself. The larger your community and the more complex your software, the harder it will be for people to stay current on what is going on. Think about the large companies or open source projects you've been a part of. How well did you know what was going on outside of your team?

As the program manager, you do the hard work of keeping track of things across the community so everyone else doesn't have to. The community should be able to come to you (or a written proxy of you) and get the latest information. *Status* can mean many things. It can refer to what teams are working on (at a high level, of course). It also can be progress towards a release schedule. Of course, it also includes dashboard-type information like bug stats.

Provide Updates, on page 31 will cover this in more detail.

Your Turn

- What venues (such as mailing lists or chat channels) do you need to monitor to keep tabs on what's going on in your community?

- What information is important to your contributors?

- Who outside your contributor community is interested in the status of the program?

Do Everything

Problem: Important tasks are left undone because a contributor became unavailable at the last minute.

Your role as a program manager means you naturally end up with a basic level of skills across much of the program. This means you can step in and be a short-term stopgap when something important isn't done. In most active open source communities, there's always more work than people to do it. At the very least, the people aren't evenly distributed across the work. Open source tends to be developer-heavy, so you might have plenty of coders and maybe even enough testers. But do you have enough people doing marketing, documentation, web design, and all of the other noncoding tasks? What's currently not being done in your community?

As the program manager, you'll often find yourself jumping in to help with something. Even if you joined a community specifically to offer your program management expertise, you'll probably end up helping out in a lot of other ways. It's only natural since you see what's going on and what's missing.

This is good. It broadens your skills, keeps the work interesting, and helps you establish credibility in the community. But beware of trying to do too much. It's not a race to collect commit bits. I often joke that if I'm pushing a commit to a repo then something has gone horribly wrong. It's good to find areas where you can make deep contributions. The important thing is to not let it overwhelm your ability to be the program manager.

Don't Take All of the Air out of the Room

Let me tell you the story of a time I messed up. I made life harder on myself by becoming a single point of failure and I denied others the opportunity to contribute.

Shortly after I became the Fedora Program Manager, I decided to join the editorial team for the Fedora Community Blog. I like writing (obviously!) and editing, and since I was producing weekly posts, it made sense that I should have publishing privileges.

But because my day job is Fedora, I was almost always the first to see review requests. It got to the point where I was editing all of the posts and the other editors eventually faded into the background. I didn't mean to end up being the sole owner of the Community Blog. It's bad for the community and bad for my ability to disconnect from work. But I ended up taking the air out of the room, so to speak. Despite my good intentions, I took a functioning team and made it dysfunctional.

Having learned from this mistake, when I became an editor of Fedora Magazine, I was intentional about giving others an opportunity to chime in. In fact, I ended up creating an "Editor of the Week" role. This person was tasked with chairing the meeting as well as being the first line of response for article proposals, comment moderation, and so on. All of the editors took turns being the Editor of the Week. As a bonus, it also solved the collective action problem where no one replied to a proposal because we were all waiting for someone else to do it.

Your Turn

- What areas of the community are you involved in that interest you? What areas do you feel like you're obligated to contribute to?

- How can you leave space for others to contribute?

- When you're making deep contributions in an area, are you keeping the broad perspective required of a program manager? If not, how can you fix that?

Manage Single Points of Failure and Burnout

Problem: Key functions in the community depend on one person.

The corollary to the previous section is that, when you're not careful, a person can accumulate responsibility until it crushes them. Even when people seem to be available at every waking moment, you never want to plan on that. For one, it's inhumane. Just as people need a break from their paid jobs, they also need a break from their unpaid jobs. And let's be honest with ourselves—significantly contributing to an open source community is an unpaid job. But it also puts your community at risk. What happens when that key person decides to finally take a vacation? Or they lose electrical service for days?

Specialization makes sense. Over time, you'll naturally see the people who can afford to be highly participatory collect more responsibility. Part of your job as the program manager is to notice when this is occurring and try to mitigate it. You may not be able to stop it, but you can at least alert people that it's happening. It's not that we don't want people to get more responsibility or gain new skills. We do! But we don't want to place the whole community on their shoulders.

Watch for cases where the same person is doing a task every time. In particular, notice when that person asks if someone wants to do a task and then does it because no one steps up. Make sure the task—including necessary permissions and dependencies—is well-documented. Try following the documentation yourself and see what's confusing or missing. Once there's good documentation, you can help recruit "apprentices" who can learn the tasks and step in when needed. You might notice someone contributing in a different area who would be a good fit. Or perhaps your contributor recruitment efforts can focus on finding someone.

This applies to you, too. It's hard to have co–program managers (although you can have program managers for specific areas), but you can at least make it so that someone can handle your work in a pinch. If "do everything but also manage single points of failure and burnout" sounds like a tough balance to strike, you're right. Welcome to program management!

Retrospective

This chapter doesn't cover everything that program management entails. That's why the rest of the book exists. But you should at least have a good sense of the role now. You see that you have to balance priorities, manage risks, communicate, and do many other tasks.

A program manager is the oil that keeps the gears turning smoothly by managing the interfaces between teams and keeping a high-level view. Doing your work well means everyone else's work gets easier, too. The next chapter zooms in a bit to make sure you have an understanding of project management.

## CHAPTER 2

Zoom in on Projects

Project management and program management are related disciplines, but with a different focus. While project management focuses on a short-term effort to produce a specific thing, program management focuses on an ongoing cross-functional effort to deliver a result. Since you're doing program management in an open source community, you'll probably find yourself spending some time on project management, too. So what's the difference?

The distinction between the two disciplines is less clear in the fluid and loosely structured context of an open source community. For example, a specific software release is technically a project within the larger program, but most communities won't draw that distinction. Given that, the chapters on schedules and features later in this book could very well be considered project management. Also, many aspects of program management are the same as in project management but zoomed out. So when you understand project management, program management makes more sense. If the teams within your community have people acting as project managers, you'll be able to understand their perspectives and language.

The Project Management Institute defines[1] project management as "the application of knowledge, skills, tools, and techniques to project activities to meet the project requirements." This is correct but entirely unhelpful. So let's build a more helpful definition.

Define "Project"

Problem: Open source projects aren't technically projects.

I have bad news for you: your project isn't a project. More accurately, the common use of "project" in open source communities doesn't match the definition

---

1.   https://www.pmi.org/about/learn-about-pmi/what-is-project-management

of "project" as used in the discipline of project management. Open source projects are actually programs, as you saw in the previous chapter. Because this chapter focuses on both disciplines, to avoid confusion it will use "project" by itself to represent the project management discipline and "open source project" to represent the program management discipline. In the rest of the book, you'll be more focused on how to put the knowledge to use, so we'll relax our strictness with the word "project."

Returning to the Project Management Institute for a moment, a project is "a temporary endeavor undertaken to create a unique product, service, or result." A few key words are important here. "Temporary" is the first one. A project has a defined end. That end may be a particular date. More likely, it's the completion of defined deliverables: the "unique product, service, or result." The other important word is "unique." If you're making something you've already made before, it's not a project. To be clear: a new release is unique in this sense because you've never made that release before. It has new features and new bugs.

Projects are composed of milestones and tasks. A milestone is a point in time where you can see how far you've come. Some milestones are decision points. Do you continue with the project or is it not worthwhile? Do you keep a particular feature in the release or move it to the next one?

Tasks are the things you do to make the project happen. Sometimes tasks are miniprojects themselves. In those cases, you decompose them until you reach the smallest reasonable task. That's generally something that takes a few hours. If you're standing up a website, installing the CMS is a task. Downloading the CMS, decompressing the code, and running the install script aren't tasks—they're too small.

Your Turn

- The line between a project and a program is sometimes blurry. Which activities in your open source community are projects? Which are programs?

- What results do the programs produce for your open source community (both the developer and user communities)?

Find the Balance

Problem: Every decision you make is a trade-off, but you're not sure what's being traded.

Fundamentally, project managers make trade-offs to balance the different aspects of the project: scope, time, cost, and quality. The first three are often referred to as the "iron triangle." This is a poor metaphor for two reasons. First, it is supposed to reflect the fact that changing one will change the other two. Your project can be done fast and cheap, but it'll be small. Or it can be massive in scope and done quickly, but that will cost a lot. But iron isn't known for being particularly flexible. If you make a triangle out of iron, you don't get to adjust it.

Secondly, quality is left out. You can adjust quality independently of the other aspects to some degree—automated testing is nearly free in some cases, and iterative development will generally improve quality, all other things being equal. Still, the choices you make to balance the "iron triangle" will end up impacting quality one way or another. For these reasons, you may find it makes more sense to think about a fixed-length string positioned by four pegs arranged in a quadrilateral. You can move a peg closer to or further from the center, but to keep the string taut, you need to adjust one or more of the other pegs. The following figure shows what that looks like. (*Why* you'd want to keep the string taut in the first place is a philosophical question beyond the scope of this book.)

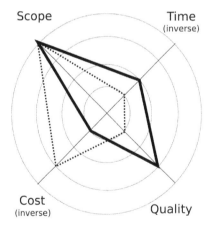

When you begin a project, you need to figure out which pegs can be moved and by how much. Ideally, all of the pegs can be adjusted as needed. More likely, one of the pegs is fixed (or nearly so). What's the most important peg for the specific project? If your last project was buggy, you might choose to focus on having a high-quality release to regain credibility with your users. So the quality peg stays still no matter how much you have to adjust the others. Or maybe the time peg has to stay still because a dependency reaches its end of life soon and you have to ship a new release with the supported version by then. For example, if your application was written in Python 2, you wanted to release the Python 3 version before Python 2 was sunsetted on January 1, 2020.

Avoid fixing two or more pegs. Two fixed pegs give you little flexibility to adjust to issues as they arise. Three fixed pegs are essentially the same as four since you won't be able to move the fourth peg and keep the string taut. But the fixed peg doesn't have to be the same from project to project only because the projects are related (like in subsequent releases of a software package). Using the examples from the previous paragraph, you may have had to sacrifice some quality to get the Python 3 version out on time. So in the next release, you'd focus on quality.

After you've determined which peg is fixed, you should evaluate how much ability you have to shift the others. For example, you can stretch the time peg out to infinity, but at some point, your project turns into "vaporware." There's probably a reasonable boundary for how much you can move it. Knowing how much room you have to move the peg allows you to make the right decisions when you need to adjust the balance. Of course, this isn't an exercise limited to the beginning of the project. Throughout the life of the project, you'll need to re-evaluate not only the balance but also which peg is fixed and what the range is for the others.

Scope

A project's *scope* is the work to be done. You often express this in terms of features to be added or requirements to be met. In corporate projects, the scope is generally dictated by business needs (including customer demands and regulatory mandates). The *project sponsor*—the manager or executive who "owns" the project—dictates the scope. The project team may have to do some analysis to figure out the requirements and features that define the scope in usable detail, but they're not setting it. The project's scope is top-down.

In open source projects, the scope is almost never top-down. Have you ever been a part of an open source community where someone tells you "okay, this is what you're working on this week, whether you like it or not"? Sure, projects may have some form of leadership role, but they're not dictating the scope. Instead, the community determines the project's scope. More specifically, the people who will be doing the work determine the scope. This is both a benefit and a challenge.

A self-determined scope helps an open source project because if people are choosing the work they do, they're likely to work on something that interests them. They'll be more excited and feel a greater sense of pride in the work. This, you hope, would lead to better code. On the other hand, if "un-fun" work needs to be done, it might not happen. Thankfully, humans aren't all alike and what one person finds mind-numbingly boring, someone else may find interesting. But if a project depends on some work that is generally considered boring, you need to find someone who either enjoys it or is willing to do it for the sake of the project, or you need to find a way to do without it.

Of the four pegs, scope is generally the most easily moved. You can shave it down to practically nothing. Of course, "we fixed a typo on the loading screen" is probably too small to be worth the effort of a project on its own. Iterative development processes make use of this by having short iterations that produce something of value at the end. Essentially, each iteration is a miniproject that results in the eventual completion of the larger project.

The value in adjusting the scope is being able to throw things overboard when you realize one of the other pegs is immovable. Perhaps the project has to be finished by a particular date—a conference, for example. You can't move the time peg any further out, but you can put aside incomplete features.

On the other hand, being the easiest peg to move isn't always in your favor. It's easy to add scope to the project, too. The project sponsor—or even the project team—can fall into the "oh, let's add this other thing while we're at it" trap. Have you ever been a part of a project where people kept adding new features? Adding the thing may be the right decision, but it still increases the scope. Do that too much and you suddenly find yourself with a much bigger project than you planned. The fact that you can add scope almost invisibly—at least until it becomes *very* visible—is why we have the term "scope creep."

Time

As you'll see in the section on keeping your release schedule accurate on page 95, time isn't fixed. For open source projects, in particular, time is most often the peg that gets moved to accommodate a change in scope. Adding another feature to the release probably means taking a little longer. Time can also adjust because of a move of the quality peg. Willing to cut corners? You can shorten the timeline. Did your beta testers find more bugs than you expected? The timeline gets longer.

Of course, the time you have available is sometimes fixed. If a project is timed to land before a conference, for example, you may not be able to afford going late. In the corporate world, the timeline is often fixed because someone higher up the org chart promised delivery of the project by a certain date. Open source projects can also promise a delivery date, but the downside of missing it is generally a temporary sense of embarrassment as opposed to the loss of a major contract. For this reason, you have more flexibility with open source projects.

Time is a tricky peg to manage, though. It relentlessly marches on while also being incredibly subjective. As a result, you feel like you have plenty of it at the beginning of a project, but by the end, you're aware of every precious second that slips away. Once the time is gone, there's no getting it back. Projects that fall behind schedule will generally not get back on schedule unless you adjust one of the other pegs.

Cost

Why are we talking about cost in a book on open source? It's free, right? First, recall that this chapter is generally about project management. Second, there's no such thing as a free lunch. Ever heard of the phrase "free as in puppy"? Even if you don't have material costs to worry about, you still have an important cost to consider: time.

This "time" is different from the "time" of the previous section. That was about the passage of time on the calendar. This is about the time your contributors (or their employers) donate to your project.

For most software projects, labor is the largest cost. Managing the project's cost essentially comes down to managing the labor. Does the project have the right people at the right time? Are those people able to work efficiently or do they spend a lot of time waiting for something?

Software products have a low *marginal cost* because a software package can be sold to a thousand customers for nearly the same cost of production as selling it to one customer. Consequently, project managers are often tempted to increase the cost in order to increase the scope or quality or to decrease the time. This is a trap; don't fall into it. Fred Brooks first wrote *The Mythical Man-Month [Bro95]* in 1975, and the lesson hasn't sunk in yet. Adding more people to a late project merely makes it later.

Returning to the specifics of open source projects, you may think this doesn't matter since you're not writing paychecks to your contributors. Even if *someone* is paying them to work on your project, they're not asking you to manage the money. Hooray! Not your problem! But the time your contributors give you—especially if they're participating on a volunteer basis—is precious.

You want to make sure that you respect it and understand that it's a finite resource. Would you want to stick around a community that regularly wasted your time?

One advantage that open source projects have in this regard is that it's relatively cheap to add more people to the project. Yes, there's an effort cost in onboarding and mentoring, which isn't trivial. But if you have good infrastructure in place, you can add people relatively easily—or at least more easily than your corporate counterparts can get more budget. In this case, you can thumb your nose at Fred Brooks and get an advantage by adding more people. The trick is you need to have them work on things that don't require a lot of coordination. For example, if you pick up five new developers at a conference, they can accelerate the timeline by working on a feature no one has started on yet. If you add them to five other teams, they'll slow those teams down.

Quality

It's time to look at the fourth and final part of the "iron triangle." Quality is relatively new to the project management discipline. Perhaps it's because the teams that develop projects are often not the ones that have to use the output. When you use—or provide support to the users of—a tool, the quality is suddenly more important to you. But whatever the reason for the late start, quality is an important part of the project management process now. There are two reasons to consider quality: for yourself and for others.

Quality for yourself is about making development easier or more efficient. If you're spending half of your time fixing bugs that you previously introduced, you'll be frustrated. Sloppy or unmaintainable code can make it harder to add new features. You find yourself going back and having to refactor code—or worse, building new code on a tenuous house of cards. Besides being frustrating and demoralizing for you as a participant in the project, it's also wasteful. In a corporate project, that results in "wasted" salary. For open source projects, it's wasted time, which is a precious donation from your community. In either case, if you consider quality from the beginning, you'll save time and cost over a "write all the code and test at the end" approach. Practices such as test-driven development and Agile development help avoid putting tests off until the end.

Quality for others is what your customers see. (I use "customers" loosely here. It means anyone who is using the outcome of the project, whether they're someone who just cut a seven-figure check to your company or someone who downloaded your project off of GitHub.) This sort of quality is often invisible during the project development process. But it's important if you want to be able to do another project. If you used some software and it formatted your hard drive unexpectedly, you'd stop using it, right? You probably wouldn't come back for version 2.0. Of course, most bugs aren't that bad, but if you're spending a lot of time fixing postrelease bugs, that's time you're not spending developing the next cool thing.

Be Your Own Customer

This concept is sometimes called "eating your own dogfood" (I've also heard "drinking your own champagne," which sounds far more preferable), but the point is that you should use the software you're developing. If you use the software, you become a customer and experience all of the joys and pains that your "real" customers experience. Using the prerelease version means that you can fix the pains before they ever get released.

Open source projects have a built-in advantage here: most projects were started to fix a problem the founders experienced. New contributors join because they want to "scratch their own itch" (what is the deal with all of these dog metaphors, anyway?). Developers in open source projects will often run the latest builds of the software, not because they've been told to, but because they want to.

But what is "quality"? You may think you know, but will people agree with your definition? It's a harder question than it might seem. The International Organization for Standardization (ISO) uses this definition:[2] the "degree to which a set of inherent characteristics of an object fulfills requirements." This leaves something to be desired.

For corporate projects with a single customer, you can define a set of requirements and evaluate the project against that. As soon as there are multiple customers, that goes out the window. You can do your best to know what the customers want or simply define what you want the requirements to be. In either case, you'll find that to be a poor measure. Each customer will have divergent (and sometimes mutually exclusive) requirements for the same project.

Ultimately, you have to come up with a definition of quality that works for your specific project. It's not set in stone; if you discover that your user base sees the world much differently than you do, you can adjust. For now, I'll simply wish you good luck. In *Track and Triage Bugs* and *Set Release Criteria*, we'll return to this question and examine quality in greater detail.

---

2. https://www.iso.org/obp/ui/#iso:std:iso:9000:ed-4:v1:en

Your Turn

- Think of a project you've worked on where the balance was off. How did you know? What did you do to adjust?

- The string doesn't always have to be fixed length. For example, adding automated testing on each commit can increase quality and reduce cost (contributor's time) simultaneously. How else can you change the length of the string?

- How can you manage labor costs when the labor is donated? How do you know how much labor is going into a project? How can you make sure the labor is used efficiently and effectively?

Know the Artifacts

Problem: You know you need to document the work, but you're not sure now.

Like many disciplines, project management has a slew of associated artifacts. Part of your job is to manage key artifacts like the project charter, project plan, Gantt chart, RACI chart, decision log, and stakeholder list. You'll find these helpful as you manage the project or program.

Project Charter

Problem: There's no clear definition of why the project exists and who is involved.

The project charter lays out what the project is all about—the who, what, when, why, and how. It is the project's foundational document. The charter, despite its importance, is a short document. This is because it is written at the beginning of the project when many details are still unknown.

The first role of the charter is to authorize the project. A *project sponsor* is named. This is the leader who says "yes, do this project." Notably, they aren't necessarily involved with the daily work of the project. In a corporate environment, a sponsor will often be a director or vice president. For a community-driven project, there's often not an explicit sponsor—the community implicitly authorizes people who want to get work done to do it. Additionally, it identifies the other members of the project team.

Besides the "who?" of the project, the charter also defines the "why?" and "what?" Give the "why?" in terms of the business need. Why is this important to the community? What outcomes are expected from a successful project? The "what?" includes the deliverables and the project's requirements.

Finally, the charter specifies the "how?" of a project. It lists the high-level schedule milestones (that's technically a "when?" but work with me here). The budget and constraints are also included.

If your project is the next release of your software, you probably don't need to bother with a charter. It serves as a helpful reference for newcomers, but it also probably doesn't change much over time. The RACI chart described on page 23 is all you need there. But if you're coordinating something else—the redesign of the community's websites, for example—a project charter can be a helpful reference point. It gives everyone a common understanding of what the project is supposed to do and in what way. If you document this up front, you avoid divergent assumptions later.

Project Plan

Problem: There's no clear definition of how the project will operate.

If you took the project charter and fed it a lot of spinach, you'd get a project plan. The project plan defines how the project will be executed. It includes a more detailed discussion of the contents of the project charter. In addition, it (generally) has sections for how changes to different aspects of the project will be managed: scope, requirements, schedule, budget, and so on. It lists the key *stakeholders*—the people who will be affected by the project.

The project plan also includes plans for communication, testing, and hiring and personnel allocation. It discusses the risks to the project's success and how they'll be monitored and mitigated. If the project is defined up front (more on methodologies in the next section), it'll also include a *work breakdown structure* (WBS). The WBS is a nested, ordered list of tasks that will be performed. It generally includes who is responsible, what dates the task will start and end on, and what dependencies exist between tasks.

Formal project plans for large projects can easily be tens of pages long, if not hundreds. Project managers will often split them into multiple documents just for ease of reading. In an open source project, you're not likely to need that level of documentation. But you may find at least some of the content beneficial. For example, developing a WBS is essentially the activity of *Build a Release Schedule*. If the project will use particular chat or email channels outside of the community's usual choice, you'll want to note that here as well.

Gantt Chart

Problem: The timeline of your project and dependencies between tasks are hard to visualize.

A *Gantt chart* provides a visual representation of your project timeline. It lists the tasks down the left side. A timeline sits across the top. The scale of the timeline varies from hours for a short project to quarters for a multiyear project.

Each item in the WBS is listed with a bar to represent the duration of the task. Arrows between the bars show task dependencies. The following Gantt chart example shows what the end result looks like. Gantt charts provide a quick way to visualize the project schedule. As an added bonus, if you highlight things like major holidays and conferences, you can get a quick feel for potential schedule conflicts.

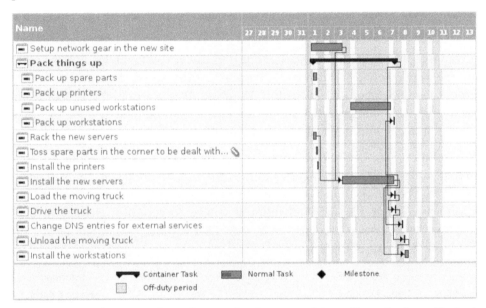

When you make your first Gantt chart, you achieve Very Serious Project Manager™ status. At least, that's the impression that I get from the reactions of developers whenever "Gantt chart" is mentioned. But like the discipline of project management in general, Gantt charts are unfairly maligned.

RACI Chart

Problem: No one knows who is responsible for which activities. Things don't get done because everyone thought someone else was going to do it.

In a large project, it's easy for you to lose track of who is responsible for each area. Someone who joins a project after it starts can have an even harder time recognizing these relationships. This can lead to tasks not getting done or decisions being made without involving the right people. The wise project manager uses a RACI chart to record this information. RACI is an acronym for "responsible, accountable, consulted, informed." But what does this mean?

- *Responsible* refers to the person or people who will actually do the work.

- *Accountable* refers to the person who "owns" the task. This person—and you generally want to have it be a single person per task—makes sure the task is done and typically has decision-making authority.

- *Consulted* means people who should provide input to decisions for this task. This might be a technical or business subject matter expert or a key stakeholder for the project.

- *Informed* refers to the people who should be told about decisions and status.

A common way to make the actual chart is to list the tasks (at a high level, not for the whole WBS) down the left side of a grid and put the names of each project team member across the top. Then you fill in a letter—R, A, C, or I—in each grid. This works well enough for small, well-defined teams. In open source projects, you don't always have small, well-defined teams.

One solution is to use roles across the top instead of specific people. I prefer to instead use the four categories across the top, as shown in the following example. Then you fill in the names in each square. The advantage of this approach is that it's more obvious if you've forgotten to make anyone responsible or accountable for a task. The disadvantage is that it's harder for a person to see all of their tasks.

	Responsible	Accountable	Consulted	Informed
Redesign project logo	Dylan Designer	Paul Projectmanager	Tina Trademarkattorney	MyCoolProject community
Add logo to project website	Wanda Webmaster	Paul Projectmanager		
Add logo to UI	Frances Frontendengineer	Paul Projectmanager		
Print new stickers	Carlos Community-manager	Paul Projectmanager	Sally Shippinclerk	Conference booth staffers

As you can see, not every task needs someone to be consulted or informed. And you can use roles instead of specific people in some places. But the accountable section should be one specific person.

No matter how you organize your RACI chart, having one is a big benefit to your project. It gives the community a shared understanding of who is responsible for what and helps to make sure no one is inadvertently left out of a decision.

Decision Log

Problem: People who join the project later—or future versions of yourself—don't know what was decided and why. Already-decided questions are reasked and waste time with moot discussion.

To remember what decisions you made and why you made them, the simple answer is "write them down." The artifact where you record this is called a *decision log*. Include who made the decision, when they made it, and what was decided. Optimally, you also list the rationale and what options were considered and rejected. This document helps prevent rearguing decisions after you've made them. Plus, it can help new contributors come up to speed by providing a summary of how you got to the present state.

Stakeholder List

Problem: You can't remember who is involved in the project.

As with other important details about a project, you should log the stakeholders—the people with some kind of vested interest in the project. Because every individual is different, you need to work with them in slightly different ways. Some people like to be spoken to directly. Others need you to couch your opinions in a more indirect manner. Keep a list of key stakeholders and their interests or communication needs and you'll interact with people in the most effective way.

Keep Your Notes Secure

 It helps you to have a document where you can say "Ben is a real jerk. Don't say anything bad about breakfast foods around him." You don't want the wrong person to see that document, particularly if they're the subject of the notes. Guard this document like you would your passwords.

Know Your Audience

In a past role, I managed the support engineering team for a small software company. Although we were a tiny company, we had a lot of "too big to fail" customers. As I wrote this section, I thought of one person I had worked with as a key customer. He was nice and understanding…unless his internal customers were on the phone, too. In that case, he was a real jerk. I suppose that for the sake of his company's internal politics, he had to be seen as defending the company against the mistakes of the vendor. With him, I had to be very careful about what information I gave him one-on-one and what information in front of others. His reaction to the same information would be different depending on whether there's an audience or not.

At another customer, their project lead was easy to get along with, but she didn't like ambiguity. My natural communication style is to reflect uncertainty, even when I feel fairly certain. I don't like being wrong, so I'll leave the door open for the unanticipated or say "should" instead of "will." She wanted certainty, so I had to learn to adjust my words to be more confident. Unless I was truly uncertain, I used a more deterministic phrasing. This saved us a lot of unnecessary back-and-forth.

For a third and final example, I had a customer contact who was big into college sports. I'm a big college sports fan myself, but his alma mater is in a different conference than mine, so I didn't always know how they were doing. I made a point of checking the latest scores for his team before I'd join a call with him. We often spent a minute or two at the beginning talking about how his football or basketball team was doing. This helped our working relationship tremendously.

In all of these cases, I had notes for myself on how to best interact with them. When I went on vacation, I made sure the teammates who would cover for me had access to the notes as well. This helped them avoid potential pitfalls when working with someone unfamiliar.

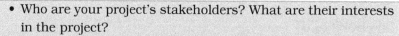

Your Turn

- Who are your project's stakeholders? What are their interests in the project?

- Open source projects rarely have a formal charter. What documentation already exists in your community to draw from? What's missing or assumed?

- Think of the people you had to work with for a while before you could effectively communicate with them. What do you wish you knew sooner?

Retrospective

This chapter condenses a large body of knowledge into a handful of pages. *Manage It! [Rot07]* by Johanna Rothman goes into much greater depth if you find yourself wanting more. But for now, it's enough that you understand the basics of project management. You learned about the triple constraint that's actually a quadruple. You understand project life cycles and methodologies. And you know a few of the artifacts that get produced when managing a project. Now we can return to the matter at hand—managing the program.

## CHAPTER 3

Communicate and Build Relationships

As you read in the section *Take the Big Picture View*, program management is concerned with the interfaces between teams. You can distill the work you do as a program manager into two C words: communication and collaboration. "Cool" is an optional addition. In this chapter, we'll explore how you communicate and build relationships with your community. Those two concepts may seem separate, but you'll see that they're inextricably linked.

Build Relationships

Problem: You're new to the role of program manager (or even to the entire project) and you don't have relationships with members of the community.

Open source projects are made of people. To work with people successfully, you'll have to build relationships with them. This means connecting on an individual basis—you can't build a relationship with the entire community at once because the community is a collection of individuals. Think about every job you've had. How much more productive are you once you've established relationships with your coworkers? Open source projects are like that, but more so; there's much less of a structured hierarchy that grants positional authority. In this section, we'll look at how to build those key relationships.

Understand Trust

Problem: You're not clear about the role of trust in open source.

Open source communities run on trust. This is true in any organization, of course, but in a company, the organizational structure gives some people authority based on their role. Let's call that "unearned" authority since it is bestowed on them from day one. (Hopefully, they've earned their way into the role that gives them the authority, but that's not important to this discussion.) In an open source community, authority is entirely "earned." The community runs on norms, not rules, so if you haven't earned trust (and thus authority), people might just ignore you.

To build that trust, you have to build connections. Trust doesn't transfer from person to person. Just because the previous program manager was well-respected, that doesn't mean you'll be respected on day one. Trust also doesn't transfer from role to role. You may have been a beloved QA lead, but you're an unknown quantity when it comes to being the program manager.

Of course, you're not always starting from zero. The trust (or distrust) built by your predecessor can give you a head start (or put you at a disadvantage). If the previous program manager did a good job, you won't have to convince the community of the benefits of the role, just that you specifically will be good in it. The reputation you develop in other communities (or other roles within your community) can give you a higher baseline. Trust, then, is a result of both your personal reputation and the reputation of your role.

Connect to the Community

Problem: You don't know the members of your community and—more importantly—they don't know you.

So now that you understand why trust is important, how do you build it? The first step is to connect with the community. You have to build interpersonal relationships.

Hopefully, you'll rarely go into a program management role without knowing the community at all. If you have experience in a community before you become the program manager, that gives you some existing cultural knowledge and lets contributors get to know you a bit. But in a large community, moving into a program management role will expose you to subcommunities that you haven't worked with before. It's important that you build connections with those parts—get to know them and let them get to know you.

There's nothing particularly ground-breaking here. You've been making friends your whole life. Open source contributors are people, just like anyone else. Connect with them as people. Spend some time listening to them. What are they working on? What challenges do they face? Do you have similar tastes in music or movies? You don't have to focus the conversation on the project—it's often better if you don't. You're trying to connect to them as a person, not as a role in the community.

Don't underestimate the power of buying someone a cup of coffee. Everyone has different motivations for participating in open source communities, but money is often not the most important. A small gesture of recognition can go a long way. Spending a few dollars on a drink is a nice gesture. When you sit down together for a few minutes to drink your beverages, you have an environment for the kind of informal chat that builds your relationship with that person.

Build Credibility

Problem: The community doesn't trust you in the program manager role.

When you're starting out as the program manager, the community doesn't have any trust in you. It's not that they *distrust* you, there's simply an absence of trust. Now that you've established some relationships within the community, you can work on the second part of building trust: building credibility. (In reality, you'll be doing both in parallel. You'll be in different stages with different people and groups. But for clarity, we're discussing connecting to the community and building credibility separately.)

You know how when you take a glass baking dish out of the refrigerator, you let it come to room temperature first so that it doesn't shatter when you put it in the hot oven? That's pretty good advice for approaching the early days of your tenure as a program manager. Your job will sometimes involve telling people "no" or "that's not how this process works" and the like. Early on, you want to be judicious with that. Go out of your way to help people so that they come to see you as being helpful, not officious. Over time, you can increase your willingness to say "no."

Another way to build credibility is to be good at your job and do it publicly. Competence is important, but it needs visibility. You don't need to brag, but you want to make sure the work you're doing is visible. Don't shy away from talking about what you do. The community can't give you credit for your work if they don't know about it. This leads to the communication discussion later in the chapter.

Competence doesn't mean you never make mistakes. If I had a dollar for every time I made a mistake when sending an email or running a script to process bugs, I'd have a lot of dollars. Everyone makes mistakes, so people tend to be forgiving if you own up to it. Apologize when you make a mistake and do your best to make it right. You'll also help your credibility when you address your mistakes proactively instead of waiting to see if someone notices them.

Although you can't directly transfer trust from one community to another, you can give yourself a credibility boost by developing a good reputation outside the community. One way would be writing a field-defining book that everyone loves and buys many copies of (hint hint!). Speaking at conferences, blogging, and appearing on podcasts are other ways to build credibility outside of your work in a particular community. It's self-promotion, for sure, and it might feel a little uncomfortable, but you can't be known as an expert if you're not known.

Communicate

Problem: Information isn't flowing from one part of the community to the others.

Now that you've developed relationships in the community, it's time to shift your focus to communication. Information is abundant in an open source project. The difficulty is that it's often unorganized and hard to find. This is where you can make a big difference and provide a huge benefit to the whole community.

Lurk Everywhere

Problem: You're not sure what's going on in the community.

To communicate information, you first have to know it. People will sometimes come and tell you what's going on in their part of the community. But mostly, you'll need to find things out for yourself.

How? Actively paying attention to all parts of the community is a full-time job—or more than one in a large community. But passively paying attention is generally manageable. That means subscribing to a lot of mailing lists (or forum topics, or whatever), issue trackers, and so on. You should also be in a lot of chat rooms.

You don't have to actively participate in these venues, or even read all of the words. Often, it's enough to skim the subject lines of emails. You're not looking for details, you're after the high-level view. It can be enough to know the general mood of the conversations. Is the team feeling good or are they in a bit of a panic? Or are they completely inactive? Of course, if something catches your eye, you can dig deeper.

When you're first getting started, you should try to show up to every team's meeting at least once, even if you won't be participating regularly. This is an opportunity to see how the team works and get a sense of where to look in the future. It's also a reminder to the team that you exist and they should let you know about important things.

Centralize Information

Problem: Other people in the community don't know where to find information.

By lurking everywhere, you collect a lot of information. But that information doesn't help anyone if you hoard it. You have to make the information available to others. The larger a project gets, the more difficult it is to know where to turn for key information. This makes your job harder, but by doing it, you make everyone else's job easier.

The idea of one dashboard to rule them all is appealing, but it never works out that way. If you try to represent all of the project's key information on a single page, you'll have an incomprehensible mess. But you can have a single page that links to the important information. The value you provide is less about knowing the information and more about knowing how to find it. If the community knows they can get to what they need from your dashboard, they don't have to remember all of the other places. And they'll see links to information they didn't even know they could get.

Besides being information overload, mega-dashboards also have the problem of needing to pull from many unrelated sources. This is likely true for your project, too, even if you're using a platform like GitLab or GitHub for your development. Sure, you could write code to automate building a dashboard (or several) from all of those information sources, but then you have to operate it. Don't underestimate the power of a manually updated dashboard. The community doesn't need up-to-the-second information, just something that's "recent enough."

For example, once a week I publish a "Friday's Fedora Facts" post on the Fedora Community Blog. It includes some bug counts from Bugzilla queries that I bookmarked, upcoming meetings, announcements, upcoming schedule milestones, and so on. This essentially functions as a dashboard, with some room for improvement. A once-per-week snapshot is sufficient most of the time. As we approach release milestones, people can follow the link to the blocker bug tracker if they want the current release blocker information.

Provide Updates

Problem: People don't check the dashboard.

You build a dashboard and no one comes. Or at least some people don't. People won't always "pull" the information you want them to have. From time to time, you'll have to push updates so that key information gets in front of the right people. Although everyone can, in theory, see all of the updates because open source communities take place in public view, you have two main audiences for these updates: people inside the community and people outside the community.

Whichever the audience, you have to assume that both audiences will see it. Working in an open source project means working in the open. This means you want to be careful about what you say. Try to take a marketing or public relations view of the message. That's not to say you should lie or be misleading, but you should consider how the message will be heard and interpreted. The Fedora Linux schedule includes both "early target date" and "target date #1" milestones, both of which are considered to be "on time." The early date is an optimistic goal for contributors to aim for so that they can hit the actual target date. But until we started drawing that distinction, people took hitting "target date #1" as a late release.

Of course, you also want to avoid being insulting or overly cynical. "We're going to be late because our code stinks and we can't run a CI environment to save our lives" might be reasonably understood as hyperbole on an internal mailing list. When that gets out—and it will if your project has a large following—the "our code stinks" part will be what people hear. It'll frame the messaging from there on. And even joking insults among people who have known each other for years don't always appear that way to outsiders. Your project's communication—and yours in particular because of the outsized role you play in communicating—tells prospective contributors what it's like to be a part of your community. Make sure it's welcoming.

Internal Updates

When sending updates to an internal audience, you don't need to provide a lot of extra context. You can assume the audience has some knowledge of the project and processes already. Of course, the larger the project, the less universally true this will be. Still, the updates can mostly be short reminders or summaries of changes, with pointers back to the main source of information. The messages for the internal audience are mostly future-facing, with some recent past thrown in the mix. You'll want to send reminders—sometimes multiple—of upcoming deadlines. As a release approaches, send regular status updates: release-blocking bugs, test status, and so on. If the schedule changes or a decision is made on shipping the release, announce those as well.

The eternal question is "how often do I send updates?" No matter what frequency you choose, it'll be too much for some people and not enough for others. Particularly for email updates, people seem to be sensitive to feeling like you're spamming them. Keep the update venue in mind: both the traffic and the type. Email is a push medium; the same volume of messages will *feel* more frequent compared to a forum or a blog. But on a high-volume mailing list, you might need a higher frequency just to avoid messages getting buried.

The best approach is to have a low-volume push venue for announcements—an announcement mailing list or a special forum category. Set the expectation that if a message goes to that venue, people in the community will read it. To keep that expectation valid, you have to be judicious about what you post. Use it for key deadline reminders, release status changes, and messages the community needs to act on. For routine status updates, use a high-volume mailing list, a blog, or a regular forum category—places where people can easily find the update if they want it, but can also easily ignore it if they don't.

External Updates

Updates for external audiences tend to be focused on the past, with a little bit of "here's what's coming next" (for example, announcing that you just shipped the latest release). This is particularly interesting (you hope!) to the tech press. These updates can also be more mundane progress updates such as we fixed X bugs, Y people contributed, and so on. If your community has a corporate sponsor, the sponsor may want those kinds of updates on a regular basis. Downstream projects may want to get these updates as well.

Whether the external updates are exciting or mundane, you don't want to assume the reader has much knowledge of the community and how it works. The usual rules of clear communication apply: avoid jargon, spell out acronyms and initialisms on first use, provide plenty of supporting links, and so on. You don't just want to give the reader the background context, you want to make it clear why they should care about the update. What does it mean for the things they care about? If you're giving numbers, add a sentence or two of editorial opinion.

Retrospective

Your success as a program manager depends on your ability to develop relationships in the community and communicate with people on the inside and the outside. Like any other skills worth having, these will take practice. The information in this chapter pointed you in the right direction. Now it's up to you to act. If you spend time reflecting on your missteps, you'll find this becomes easy in short order.

## CHAPTER 4

Make Good Decisions

One of the more challenging aspects of any leadership role in an open source project is the act of making a decision. Open source communities work in the open and have many different viewpoints to balance. You're not going to make everyone happy, but following a predictable and fair decision-making process can help you avoid making the community angry.

You make hundreds of decisions a day, mostly without thinking about them. You decide what to have for lunch, which email to reply to first, what to name the iterator in your for loop, and so on. This chapter isn't about those small decisions. In the next few pages, you'll develop a process for making big, project-impacting decisions. We'll focus on the process of making a decision with a specific proposal. If you're trying to have an open brainstorming session, you can do that as an open discussion in your usual venue (for example, the development mailing list). You may still want to define the problem clearly, but let the solution emerge from the discussion. Once a specific proposal coalesces from the vapors of open discussion, you can apply the information from the rest of the chapter.

Define the Question

Problem: What's being decided is unclear.

The first step in making good decisions is to know what you're deciding. This sounds obvious—and it is!—but it gets overlooked far too often. How many times have you been in conversation with someone only to discover that you're not talking about the same thing? Most consequential decisions in an open source community are made by a group, which means the group has to have a shared understanding.

Identify the Problem

To develop a shared understanding, identify the problem. Why do you need to make a decision in the first place? Is the release at risk of being delayed? Are you trying to improve the security of your code repository? Do you have a thousand t-shirts sitting in boxes waiting to be given away? Whatever it is, you have to be clear on the reason you need a decision.

Not all problems are bad. Having a thousand t-shirts to give away can be a good problem. It means your community is large enough to justify someone spending the money to buy a thousand t-shirts. Sure, figuring out an equitable way to distribute the shirts is *hard*, but it's a good problem to have. It's still a problem to solve, though.

To identify the problem, you need to be able to articulate *what* you want to change and *why*. The *how* isn't important yet. There's no secret trick to knowing these two things. The very fact that you're trying to make a decision suggests that you already know. It's sharing what you know that moves you forward.

Be clear about what you see as the problem. If you say "we should improve the project's security," some people might think you want to change the compiler flags used to build the project. What you're actually worried about is someone compromising a developer account and inserting malicious code. If instead, you say "we should protect against developer account compromises because our enterprise users are becoming more concerned about supply chain attacks," everyone knows what you mean.

When you identify the problem, you're not guaranteed unanimous support. Not everyone will agree that the problem is worth solving. They may take issue with your reasoning and insist that what you call a problem is actually a key benefit. That's okay. At least now the discussion has a shared understanding.

Develop a Proposal

After you've identified the problem, it's time to find a solution. To start this process, make a concrete proposal. Don't say "we should keep our repository access up-to-date." That's vague, and the implementation details can vary greatly, resulting in a lot of "I never agreed to *that*!" Instead, propose something like "in order to protect against malicious code insertion from account compromise, at the beginning of every release cycle, the security officer will check all accounts with commit access and remove anyone who has been inactive for more than six months." This makes it clear to everyone what's to be decided.

One thing you probably noticed about the example in the previous paragraph is how specific it is. It directly references the problem you identified. It answers the questions of "why?", "when?", "who?", and "what?" You could also argue that "the repository" is an implied answer to "where?" The question of "how?" isn't addressed because that's an implementation detail to figure out later (although if you know the "how?" to a reasonable degree, then you might as well include it).

If you recall learning about composition in grade school, these questions will sound familiar. The reasoning hasn't changed: you're trying to make sure your reader understands what you're writing. People will guess—often subconsciously—at the answers to any of the questions you don't specifically address, which can result in major differences in understanding. Not every proposal requires an explicit answer to every question. For example, "all accounts with commit access must have two-factor authentication enabled" is sufficiently clear. But in general, the more questions you can answer in a proposal, the better agreement you'll have as to what's being decided.

Write Proposals When You Have Strong Opinions

Proposals don't spring forth out of thin air; someone has to write them. If you have a strong opinion on the path forward, the best way to give it a head start is to write a proposal. Blank pages are hard, and people will generally prefer batting around a strawman instead of coming up with something themselves. Even if your proposal isn't accepted as-is, you shape the discussion by giving it a starting point.

Give a Voice

Problem: The community doesn't feel like they have input on decisions.

One of the great joys and challenges of open source communities is the lack of a fixed hierarchy. Great ideas can come from anywhere, which makes open source projects vibrant and innovative. But that also means that community members expect to be able to have their say on any issue. You don't have to follow all of the suggestions—some of them are bound to be mutually exclusive anyway—but you do need to give the community a voice.

Not Everyone Gets a Voice

It's okay to scope the boundaries of who gets a voice on a given decision. For example, if you're thinking about changing the default database back end for your project, you might want input from contributors and users alike. On the other hand, if you're trying to decide what time to hold the QA team meeting, you only care about the input from people who would show up. You can expect that others may chime in anyway, but you don't have to take their input into account.

There are two main reasons to give a wider audience a voice. The first is that your idea isn't perfect. Giving others who are invested in the decision the opportunity to provide their own ideas can only help. Often, you'll find that you haven't considered a particular angle. The different perspectives others provide test the assumptions of your idea before you take any steps to implement it.

The second reason to give a voice is that it helps the community accept the end result. In his talk on expectations versus agreements,[1] business coach Steve Chandler says that people will rebel against expectations, but will honor agreements. Like any other negotiation, an agreement does result in exactly what you want, but it provides a mutually acceptable outcome. When you make people feel like they've been heard, they're more likely to go along with the ultimate decision. They might reserve the right to say "I told you so" later, but they won't actively undermine the decision.

To give a voice, you have to answer three questions: "who?", "how?", and "when?" "Who?" is the group that gets to provide input. You generally want to draw this as wide as possible so that you don't shut out potential good ideas or make contributors feel excluded. On the other hand, don't feel like you have to listen to every opinion simply because it's offered. As noted in the previous tip, you can decide where to draw the line.

"How?" refers to the method that people will use to provide their input. You might announce a poll on a mailing list but ask that people provide their input by voting in the poll and not by posting to the list. Or you might announce a proposal on several lists for wider visibility but ask that all discussions happen on one list. In general, you want feedback to be provided publicly and in one specific list so the community can engage with each other.

---

1. https://www.youtube.com/watch?v=Ajz5ddoL_Ww

If the discussion is happening in your inbox or on two different mailing lists and a social media platform, it's hard to piece everything together.

Last, "when?" lets everyone know how long they have to provide input. Although most decisions are reversible and can be revisited, you don't want to be constantly discussing the same topic for months on end. Setting a deadline sets an expectation for when the feedback window closes and the decision-making process moves forward. A week is a nice, round window that gives people an opportunity to weigh in a time or two. You can extend it to multiple weeks for more important decisions. Sometimes people are tempted to wait until the discussion dies down, but this lets one or two people essentially filibuster your process. Honestly, in most cases, after a week or two have passed, whatever discussion continues is either a tangent, repetitive, or people talking past each other. Set a time limit and stick to it.

Take a Vote

Problem: There's no clear method for making a decision.

After you've given the community a voice, it's time to make the decision by taking a vote. Much like with giving a voice, you have to answer the "when?", "who?", and "how?" "When?" is the easiest question to answer, so let's start there. Keeping the vote open for a week is a good starting point. Hopefully, everyone has had time to keep up with the discussion. If they haven't, they have a week to catch up. If the discussion period is more than two weeks, you might consider going with a voting period that's half of the discussion period, but in most cases, you'll find that a week is sufficient. Of course, you can make exceptions for cases that require an emergency decision, but these are rare.

The answer to "when?" should rarely be "in a meeting." That leads to exclusionary decision-making that privileges contributors who can be around at the right moment. In a global community with volunteer contributors, that subset of contributors is going to be small. For nonemergency decisions, only make the decision in a meeting if *both* of the following are true: the proposal has had a full public discussion period and everyone who has a vote is present. Otherwise, you can take votes in the meeting—or formalize the decision if asynchronous voting has already occurred—but don't *make* the decision in the meeting.

"Who?" is the next question you have to answer. This will depend on the decision's context and the community norms. For example, the decision on whether or not to accept a feature proposal could be a decision for the technical steering committee, while the decision to move to a new Git forge might be a matter for everyone with commit permission to decide. In any case, it's critical that you make clear who gets to vote from the beginning of the process—and that you can justify the reasoning.

In general, you want to keep the voting group small. This isn't to be exclusive, it's to be expedient. The feedback received from the community needs to be discussed and digested, and bigger groups will take longer to do that. If voting is limited to a particular team and the team is relatively small—perhaps 20 members or fewer—then letting everyone vote is reasonable. If you have a large number of people who could potentially vote, it's better to vest that authority in a representative body. Voting for members of that body might be open to the community at large, but the representatives cast votes on individual decisions.

Last, we come to answering "how?" Laying out all of the options would be a book in itself, so let's stick with a few basics. Open source projects don't have the tools of governments—armies, taxation, police forces, and so on—that carry the power of life and death, so we can afford to keep things simple.

The best form of voting is no vote at all. A person has an implicit or explicit authority to make the decision in the scope of their role in the project. As the program manager, you're responsible for building the project schedules, so you get to decide what tool to use. You might—particularly if you're hoping to have others contribute to the schedule—solicit feedback on the tool from the community. But it's ultimately your call. This is a common form of decision-making in open source projects. Essentially, you're saying to the community "hey, I'm planning on doing a thing, please tell me if you see something wrong with my plan."

Sometimes, though, you need a little more formality. In this case, you'll have people casting votes. The exact mechanism can vary, but the most common form is a +1 (approval), -1 (disapproval), or 0 (abstention) in a ticket or meeting. This seems simple, but the options for what we do with the numbers get interesting.

One option is to require full consensus: proposals are only approved with unanimous agreement. A full consensus model has the benefits of having buy-in from everyone. Proposals approved by full consensus have been likely modified a few times to be the best they can be. On the other hand, full consensus also means a single person can hold back a proposal indefinitely. This can frustrate the community and prevent important technical or cultural changes.

Another option is to let the majority win. This means if a proposal gets more +1 votes than it does -1 votes, it is approved. The majority wins model avoids the roadblock issues that come with full consensus. But for particularly contentious proposals, a close vote may cause a rift in the community. If a proposal to switch development frameworks passes by a single vote, those in the minority may decide to fork the project. Forks aren't always bad, but a contentious fork tears the community apart.

Somewhere in between is a hybrid approach, where the net vote has to be above a certain threshold. For example, you might require proposals to have a net score of +3 to pass. A proposal that receives +5 and -4 wouldn't pass because the net is +1, but a proposal that receives +6 and -3 would because the net is +3. A net score threshold system avoids the roadblocks of a full consensus approach while still requiring a loose consensus in order to approve a proposal. The weakness here is that if you don't have enough people casting votes, the proposal will languish. A proposal with two +1s and no other votes won't pass if the threshold is +3.

But what do you do with votes that aren't +1 or -1? If someone votes 0 or doesn't vote at all, how does that factor in? In general, you should ignore nonvotes—calculate the votes based on the number of votes actually cast. Many open source contributors participate on a volunteer basis, and sometimes they can't cast a vote. Or maybe they don't feel qualified to vote on a particular proposal. Don't block proposals because a volunteer disappeared for a few weeks. As for the votes of 0, treat them arithmetically. In other words, if a proposal has two +1s, one -1, and eight 0s, the net vote is +1. If you're operating on a majority wins model, then the proposal passes.

Avoid Overcomplicated Voting

 We have a tendency in open source projects to overcomplicate the decision process. Unlike in code, the voting system doesn't need to handle every conceivable exception. I've seen conversations where people argued in favor of distinguishing between a vote of "0" and a vote of "present," where the former would be counted for determining what constitutes a majority of votes and the latter wouldn't. For a group that almost always reaches a unanimous conclusion, this is a wholly unnecessary complication. Unless votes are routinely mired in contentious arguments over how to add the numbers, stick to the simple solution. The longer it takes to explain how votes are tallied, the wronger your system is.

Retrospective

You've now learned about the importance of clearly defining the problem and the proposed solution. You have a clear understanding of the difference between having a voice and getting a vote. Now you're ready to make good decisions in your community. Even if the decision itself turns out to be wrong, you know that you followed the right process to make it.

You may have noticed we didn't discuss governance structures. That's generally not up to the program manager, although you can have influence, particularly early in a community's formation. The Red Hat blog[2] and Karl Fogel's *Producing Open Source Software [Fog17]* have excellent discussions of project governance models if you want to explore the topic more.

---

2.   https://www.redhat.com/en/blog/understanding-open-source-governance-models

## CHAPTER 5

Design Suitable Processes

As a program manager, processes are your jam. You may not love them, but you recognize their value. A well-designed process improves the visibility of work, aids coordination between contributors, and provides a consistent, predictable experience for all involved. You're going to spend a lot of time involved with processes, either directly or as a consultant to teams who are working on their own processes. In this chapter, you'll learn how to design a process that fits the needs of your community without being too much of a burden.

Some people enjoy processes for the sake of processes. It gives them a sense of control in a world that often feels out of control. But by and large, contributors to an open source community aren't those people. Particularly if they're volunteering their time, contributors don't want it to feel like work. They want to do cool, fun open source things.

This isn't to say that your community won't follow any processes. They understand that cool, fun things need to follow some amount of process—even Calvinball[1] has *a* rule. You simply have to show that the process makes life better. To do that, it has to solve a problem. Let's start there.

Define the Context

Problem: You lack clarity on what problem the process is supposed to solve.

As with making decisions (see Identify the Problem, on page 36), you don't need a unanimous agreement that a problem exists, although it helps if everyone can recognize that *someone* experiences the problem. If there's no problem to solve, you don't need to create a process. If you keep this in mind, you will be less likely to create a process just because you feel obligated to have one.

---

1. https://calvinandhobbes.fandom.com/wiki/Calvinball

Set Goals

The first step in defining the context is to set the goal of the process. You state the problem but in a happy way. For example, in creating a bug triage process, your goal may be to decrease the average time to resolution by 10%. More likely, you'll not be so specific and instead set the goal to reduce the average time to resolution.

Some goals lend themselves to being measured, like our example in the previous paragraph. But that doesn't mean you need to be specific when setting the goal. The important part is the direction of the change, not the magnitude. This is good since many of the goals you might build a process for are hard to measure. For example, as you'll read in *Manage Features*, one of the goals of a feature-planning process is to improve coordination. How do you measure that? Generally, you'll know by "feel" if you're successful.

A process can—and often will—have multiple goals. Sometimes these goals are seemingly unrelated. Returning to the bug triage example, the goals can include reducing the time to resolution, improving developer efficiency, and growing the contributor community. In addition, several processes can serve the same goal. The goal of growing the contributor community can be a motivating factor for both a bug triage process and a swag giveaway process.

The goals you set for the process answer "why are we creating a process?" Almost any answer you give to that question is the right answer if it meets a need of your community. ("Because our peer projects have a process like this" is a wrong answer on its own.) The important thing is to be clear about what the goals are. This helps you get community buy-in and helps you keep the process on target as you design it.

Define the Constraints

As any parent of a young child knows, merely wanting a thing isn't enough. You can *want* to ride a pony on the moon, but that doesn't mean it can realistically happen. Open source contributors aren't children, but you can still find the community wishing for things that can't realistically happen. When designing a process, you have to keep yourself limited to the realm of the possible. This means identifying your constraints.

Some of your constraints will be *constraints of technology*. Constraints of technology are the things outside the realm of the possible. These constraints might be universally true—you'll never get your network packets to go faster than the speed of light. Others may only be true for the specific technology choices you've made—Subversion is going to be centralized, no matter how much you wish it weren't. In the latter case, you may have a valid reason for the choices that constrain you, but they still constrain you. You might decide to make changes that will remove the constraint, but for the purposes of the process you're designing now, the constraint exists.

Other constraints are *constraints of principle*. These are the things that are technically possible, but unacceptable to your community. For example, a proprietary bug tracker might meet all of your needs, but your community is committed to using only open source software. Or you might have to use a self-hosted version of an open source bug tracker because the community won't accept a software-as-a-service version outside of its direct control. Not all of the constraints of principle are technical in nature. Your community may require all contributors to agree to abide by a code of conduct or to sign a contributor license agreement. Opinions on matters of principle vary greatly between—and often within—open source communities, so it's critically important that you identify which apply to your specific community.

Now that we've established the boundaries of the realm of the possible, it's time to figure out what is probable. *Constraints of resources* are common in any community-driven project. (In fact, they're common in any project. How many times have you heard "we don't have the budget for that" in your day job?) Resource constraints often manifest as hardware limitations. You don't have enough disk space to keep every build ever produced so you have to clean up old builds after some amount of time. Or you can't build your application for mainframe computers because you don't have a mainframe available to build on. Maybe you can't have an annual contributor meeting because you don't have the funds to pay for travel for everyone. Resource constraints can generally be solved by spending money if you're not cash-constrained, to begin with. And you likely are.

The final two types of constraints are closely related: *constraints of convenience* and *constraints of time*. A time-consuming process is often, but not always, inconvenient. But because you're dealing with a largely volunteer contributor community, you have a tight budget for both inconvenience and time. If a process is too inconvenient or too time-consuming, your contributors will be more likely to find another community to participate in. Even when the time is "hidden," a process that takes too long won't be useful. If your blog editorial process takes a month, your project's commentary on the pressing issue of the day will be stale long before it is read. Every process has some kind of time constraint: there will always be *some* upper bound on when the outcome of the process is no longer useful.

Build a Process

Problem: You need to design a process to fit the problem you identified.

Now that you've set your goals and identified the constraints, it's time to build the process. You'll need to think about who does what and when. Consider how information and artifacts flow through the process. What triggers the various steps? How do certain conditions change the path?

Look for Existing Patterns

Good news! You probably don't need to invent a process from scratch. In open source, we borrow ideas from other communities all of the time. There's a good chance that someone else already has a process that does what you're after. Start with that. You can adapt it to meet your community's specific needs if you have to.

But maybe you're trying to do something no other project has done before. (At least as far as you can tell.) In that case, you're still not necessarily starting from scratch. You can look for patterns in how your contributors are already behaving. What norms have built up organically? For example, have people been sharing design documents before they start coding new features? If so, then including that as a step in the features process makes sense. At their best, processes codify existing norms to make sure they're reliably followed.

Think about roads. Some roads were planned from the beginning as part of a development. But other roads started as paths worn by travelers—whether human or animal—following a similar course repeatedly. These roads don't always follow a straight line, but they embody thousands of iterations worth of knowledge. Over time, travelers learned where the terrain was easiest and that became the road. You can build a process the same way by documenting the existing practice.

Sketch the Flow

Whether you're starting from scratch or borrowing an existing process, the next step is to sketch the flow. A "sketch" doesn't have to be an actual drawn picture—although those can help, as you'll see in a moment—a written description works, too. In fact, writing it out first can help you draw the picture, so let's talk about that first.

Writing down the flow of the process isn't the place to show off your literary chops. In fact, the closer to grade school your writing is, the better it is. Write simple sentences that are simply subject, verb, and object. Put the steps in an ordered list so you can refer to previous steps if needed. If the process has conditionals, start with one path from beginning to end. Then add in the other paths. The following example shows how you might sketch out a feature proposal process.

```
1. Feature Owner fills in proposal template.
2. Feature Owner submits proposal to Feature Wrangler.
3. Feature Wrangler checks proposal.
3a. If the proposal is complete, continue to the next step.
3b. If the proposal is incomplete, proposal returns to #1.
4. Feature Wrangler announces proposal to community.
5. Feature Wrangler submits proposal to Technical Committee.
6. Technical Committee votes on proposal.
6a. If approved, continue to the next step.
6b. If rejected, process ends.
7. Feature Owner implements proposal.
```

You may have noticed that the example doesn't say anything about how the steps happen. Where does the feature owner fill in the proposal template? How do they submit it to the feature wrangler? How long does the feature wrangler wait after announcing the proposal before submitting it to the technical committee? These are all questions to answer, but not right away. Once you've built out the skeleton of the process, you can add in those details.

Now that you have a rough sketch of the process flow, you can make actual sketches (or digital pictures if your drawing skills aren't great). Two diagrams are handy in trying to express the process: a swim lane diagram and a flow chart.

A *swim lane diagram* looks sort of like a swimming pool, hence the name. It is useful for drawing attention to who performs which steps of a process. Each lane represents one person or team, and each step appears in the appropriate lane. The image of a swim lane on page 48 illustrates the process flow for the previously discussed feature proposal.

A *flow chart* is something you may already be familiar with. It represents the movement from step to step in the process but without the emphasis on who performs the step. (Strictly speaking, then, a swim lane diagram is a type of

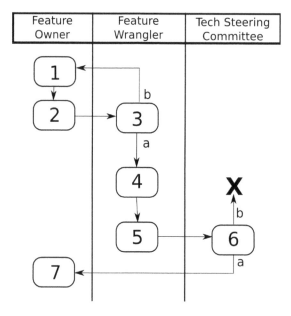

flow chart.) Because the actor is de-emphasized (or ignored entirely), flow charts are useful for representing the perspective of objects. For example, the following image of a flowchart shows how a feature proposal moves through the previously described process.

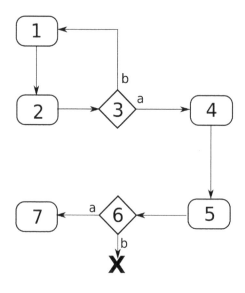

Balance Trade-offs

One of the important parts of program management, as you know, is finding the right balance. When you're designing a process, you have to balance the trade-offs between different options. The process you might design in an ideal world where you have unlimited resources and everyone loves you looks different from what you design here in the real world where you have hardly any hardware or money to throw at the problem and participants are often unenthusiastic about the process.

As you're balancing these trade-offs, you need to compare the benefits and the costs. But you can't just do a straightforward cost-benefit analysis. Cost-benefit analysis, as typically done in the business world, looks at costs and benefits in aggregate across the organization. That won't work in an open source community. First, you can't convert everything to a dollar amount. Second, and more importantly, open source communities aren't as "sticky" as a job where someone gives you a paycheck for participating. Contributors care about the overall health of the community, of course, but if a process is a net benefit to the community but a net detriment to them, they're not likely to put up with it.

The cost-benefit analysis here isn't about adding up positive and negative numbers and getting a single answer. Instead, it's a matter of looking at what the costs and benefits are and to whom they apply. This allows you to be intentional in your choices. It's okay to design a process that benefits some participants more than others—in fact, most processes work that way. But you should be aware of that choice so that you can try to be fair on the whole.

Balancing the costs and benefits happens throughout the process, but having the diagrams in the previous section can help point out places where there's an undue cost. For example, if your swim lane diagram shows one person acting in a process three times, you can look to see if those steps can be placed consecutively. This way, the person can do all of their actions in one fell swoop and then hand off the results to the next person. In general, the more complex the diagram is, the more costs are being imposed. (Unfortunately, the opposite doesn't hold true. A simple diagram can still have costly steps.)

Now that you have a thorough understanding of the trade-offs you're balancing, go back to your process skeleton and start filling in the details. Include where or how people perform their steps. Take note of dependencies between steps and add in waiting periods, if appropriate.

Implement the Process

Problem: You need to put the process into action.

Congratulations on designing a magnificent process. You built a process by sketching an initial draft from existing patterns, balancing trade-offs, and filling in details. Now it's time to turn it loose on the world. But wait! Before you fully implement the process, you'll want to give it a test run. This is essentially user-acceptance testing, but for processes instead of software. (Of course, your process may involve new software, so it's sometimes also user-acceptance testing for software, too.)

To test the process, you'll want to find a few people to give it real-world usage. As the designer, you're too close to the process to evaluate it fairly. Plus, you're probably not the only person who'll participate in the process, so you might not have the perspective of people who participate in a different role. You'll want to get someone with experience in the community, particularly in the context that they'll use the process. (A long-time documentation contributor, for example, might not give you the best feedback on a release engineering process if they've not participated in release engineering activities.) They should be able to give the process a fair shake. You don't want someone who is hostile to the process testing it out, but you do want someone who'll tell you which parts don't work.

Testing Wrecks the Project but Saves the Day

Fedora's Changes process (our version of the process described in *Manage Features*) uses wiki pages as the data store. It involves a lot of copying and pasting as well as naïve attempts to scrape and parse those pages in scripts. This was error-prone and inconvenient (at least for me), so I decided to try something new. I set up a kanban board with plenty of custom fields on each card to make the proposals more parseable. Over the course of a summer, I mentored a student as he wrote automation to handle each step of the wrangling process. We got rid of copying, pasting, and parsing essentially free-form text. Every step, post-submission happened via API calls with well-delimited data. It was a huge improvement.

Then I asked a trusted and experienced community member to give it a few test runs. That's when we discovered that the tool we'd based the work on required each custom field to be saved individually. There were 20 or so separate fields, each of which needed a click of a save button or else the input would be lost. I decided that was far too inconvenient for the developers who would be submitting proposals. Clicking the save button on each field is quick, and many would have done it habitually, but the inconvenience of lost work for those who didn't was too great. We ultimately decided to keep the status quo.

I was glad that we had done test runs before rolling the new process out community-wide. The intern and I largely used test data and were more focused on how the glue scripts worked. We didn't pay much attention to the tool we were using. Having someone else test with real-world usage highlighted flaws we hadn't noticed.

If your real-world testing brings flaws to light, go back and fix them. Once the real-world testing looks good, it's time to get the process in place for real. To do that, you'll want to have documentation.

The diagrams you developed are useful, but they're not sufficient. You also need to write out the process. Include links to tools, supporting documentation, and so on. Some document "rules" for the process are: criteria for steps, how exceptions will be handled, and what recourse is available if the process is skipped.

For the sake of posterity, you should document the reasoning behind the steps in the process. Explaining the trade-offs helps the future you avoid making a bad trade-off later. To keep the process documentation clear, don't put the "why?" documentation in the middle of the "what/how?" documentation. It's there as a historical reference for those who are interested and will distract readers who are trying to figure out how to participate in the process.

Now that you have your documentation lined up, you're ready to announce the process to the community. This being open source, you've probably been working, if not in public, at least not hidden the whole time. But people who aren't directly involved in creating the new process have largely been ignoring the work. So now's your time to introduce it. Share the documentation that you wrote. Explain the benefits. Anticipate and rebut the objections before they're expressed. You're selling the community on the new process, so pull out all of the stops.

Make Revisions

Problem: The process has diverged from what the community needs.

If you're lucky, your new process is perfect on the day you roll it out. It meets all of the goals and everyone loves it. But even a perfect process will become imperfect over time. The world around you constantly changes.

Technology shifts, changing people's preferences and what is possible. SourceForge used to be the place for hosted software releases and version control. Now GitHub is the default for many developers. In many communities, mailing lists are being supplanted by Discourse, and Internet Relay Chat is being dropped in favor of richer chat protocols. What works for your community today may be painfully archaic in a few years.

So how do you know when it's time to make changes? After all, you don't want to "fix" what isn't broken. The easiest way is to look for pain points. Do you see people complaining about particular steps of the process? Maybe they need to be changed. Are there surprises happening that the process was intended to prevent? Perhaps it needs to be adjusted or extended. For example, if new contributors aren't signing up for the mailing list that the process assumes everyone is a member of, over time fewer and fewer people will receive the messages.

The other telltale sign of a process in need of revision, apart from the wails of pain, is silence. When it's possible to do so, people will simply skip a process they don't think is valuable. If you notice that members of the community are skipping all or part of a process, you have two choices. The first is to sell the benefits of the process to the rogue. Perhaps they don't appreciate what the process does for them and the community. Alternately, you can treat it as an indication that the process doesn't add the intended value. Either one could be true, but if multiple people are skipping the process, that gives you an indication the likely answer is the latter. Remember that the process exists to serve the community; the community doesn't exist to serve the process.

Once you've determined that you need to revise the process, you go through the process in this chapter again. This time, the existing pattern that you're studying is the current process. But don't assume that the goals and constraints are still the same. If they've changed, the process built on top of them must change, too.

Thankfully, most of the time you have to revise a process, you won't need to tear the whole thing down and start from scratch. As in software development, iterative improvement is the name of the game. You make small adjustments to reflect what your community learns from using the process. For example, you might add a link to the relevant mailing list thread as part of the documentation for a feature proposal so that it's easier to find for reference later. Or you might eliminate the requirement for manual code review after your new continuous integration service is online. If you continuously tend the process, it won't need a major overhaul as often.

Retrospective

Like any skill, excellence in process design takes experience. If you take an iterative approach, you'll have plenty of opportunities to refine your earlier decisions. But if you start by clearly defining the problem and constraints, making intentional choices in trade-offs, and clearly communicating the value, you'll be off to a good start. The community may not love the process, but they'll see the benefit and will follow it willingly.

## CHAPTER 6

Hold Useful Meetings

As a program manager, your life seems to revolve around meetings. People often talk about being glad when their meetings are done so they have time to get their "real work" done. But since your job is largely communication and coordination, meetings *are* real work, and they're not the fun part, usually.

Since meetings are an inescapable part of life, we might as well be good at them. Open source projects present new and different challenges for meetings. You can't just act like it's the same as a corporate meeting. Participants are globally dispersed, are often volunteers, and can opt out with little or no consequence.

This chapter covers why meetings exist in open source projects. You'll learn how and where to schedule them and how to make sure they're useful. Finally, you'll get a reminder about how meetings affect your project's inclusiveness.

Why Bother?

Problem: You or your community don't want to have meetings. You'd rather work completely asynchronously.

Maybe you don't take "meetings are an inescapable part of life" as a given. Good for you. It's certainly true some successful open source projects—even rather substantial ones—don't have meetings. If it works for them, that's terrific. I would hate if the only reason you held a meeting was "because Ben said I should in his book."

You can get a lot of value from meetings, though. They give you the opportunity to have a more natural discussion of contentious, confusing, or complicated topics. They also serve as a good forcing function for getting work done. "I'll get this task completed before the next meeting" is much more concrete—and more likely to be done—than "I'll get this task completed." Finally, they give your contributors a chance to interact regularly, which helps your community cohesion. Let's examine each of these in turn.

Have Natural Conversations

Problem: Troubleshooting and brainstorming conversations done asynchronously take a long time and lose momentum before they're done.

Rapid iteration and exploration of thoughts require rapidity. You get that rapidity by putting people in the same (physical or virtual) space at the same time. That's fundamentally what a meeting is.

Asynchronous communication (such as email and message boards) is great for time-distributed projects. It doesn't matter if you sent the email at 3 AM Australia time because your contributors down under will be able to read it when they wake up. An asynchronous message also gives you the opportunity to think through your content and make sure everything is well-explained before you send it. But (apart from pointed blog wars of days gone by) people don't naturally communicate that way.

Think about the conversations you have. Do people take turns talking for minutes on end? Or do they say a few things, and then someone responds, and you go back and forth building off what the last person said? Okay, some conversations feel like that first one, and I'll admit I've been guilty of that from time to time. But when someone has a question about something you said, a correction, or an improvement, it's much easier to address it before you've moved on to the next part of your message. Think of it as an iterative development for ideas.

Don't take this to mean that the long written message is totally bad. I've been known to hammer out some words in my time. Heck, I'm writing an entire book right now. If that's not an endorsement of lengthy asynchronous communication, I don't know what is. But the point is that sometimes the ability to have small conversations in real time helps everyone come to a consensus much more quickly. Think about a long email thread you've been on. How well can you keep track of the different branches of the conversation when you're thirty messages in?

Fedora's blocker review process historically revolved around a weekly blocker review meeting. For up to three hours (blessedly, it was rarely this long), interested participants discussed the proposed release blockers and decided whether or not to accept them. Some proposed blockers have an obvious status, but for many, there are nuances that require discussion.

In the Fedora Linux 33 development cycle, we began using a ticket system for asynchronous voting. This lets us handle the easy cases over the course of the week so that the meeting could focus on the bugs with disagreement or confusion. As a result, the meetings got shorter which made everyone happier.

We could have ditched the meetings entirely, but the real-time discussion was too valuable. By focusing on the valuable parts and moving the straightforward pieces to an asynchronous mechanism, we made the whole process better. And, as you'll see at the end of this chapter, we made it easier for more of the community to participate.

Use Meetings as a Forcing Function

Problem: People aren't completing their assigned tasks.

Meetings present the opportunity for picking due dates. Years ago, I had the fortune to sit in on a training workshop led by Tom Limoncelli that was based on his book *Time Management For System Administrators [Lim06]*. Tom taught us a lot in that half a day, but perhaps the most important lesson was this: if it doesn't have a due date, it's not getting done. You can change the due date as many times as you need to, but it has to exist.

You're a busy person with more things to do than time to do them. If you put a due date on something, that's a way of holding yourself accountable. Some due dates, of course, are externally imposed. If you keep pushing back your payment on a utility bill, the provider will disconnect your service. If you put off buying Mother's Day flowers for your mom, eventually they'll become Father's Day flowers for your dad. But you can put off adding a new link to your website indefinitely with no real harm. Putting a due date on it, even if you don't hit the original goal, at least gives you a plan to work against.

Meetings are great for this. If you have a regular meeting cadence, putting a deadline on something is as simple as saying "by the next meeting." This can be a good option if there's not a "natural" deadline for a task (for example, a milestone on the release schedule you'll develop in *Build a Release Schedule*). If a task will take longer than the time available between meetings, you can say "two meetings from now" or "by the February 30 meeting."

Of course, wishing it were so doesn't make it happen. Particularly if contributors to your project are volunteers, they might not be able to get what they intended done. And that's okay. At least now there's accountability. If you notice a task keeps getting pushed back, maybe you can find someone else to take it.

Get to Know Each Other

Problem: Your community feels like a collection of individuals, not a cohesive team. Contributors only know each other as chat handles or email addresses, not as people.

An often-overlooked benefit of meetings is the chance to get to know fellow contributors. Meetings are—and should be!—mostly about getting business done, but there's something about real-time communication that helps you get to know a person. Jokes, idioms, and asides that might get edited out of an email spring forth. If your meeting platform supports it, participants will often chat informally while waiting for the meeting to start or after it ends.

Of course, all of this can happen in chats outside of meetings. The nice thing about a meeting is that it brings people together in the same place (virtual place, in this case) at the same time. This gives your community an opportunity to be around each other in a way that doesn't always happen in regular chat channels.

Schedule the Meeting

Problem: You're not sure when to hold a meeting. It's hard to find a time that works for everyone.

Scheduling a meeting is the most difficult task placed before a program manager. Let's see how we can make it work.

Even when you're scheduling a meeting within your company, where you can see everyone's calendars, and you all work relatively predictable hours, the odds of finding an open meeting slot drop exponentially with each additional attendee. In an open source project? Forget about it!

In addition to the time zone differences that you get in any large organization, the nature of open source contribution adds a dimension of challenge. Some people contribute as part of their day job, so they'd like to meet during "normal working hours." Others are volunteering and would prefer to meet during off-hours. Some volunteer contributors are forbidden by policy or network rules from contributing during work hours even if they wanted to. So even within a single time zone, you're probably out of luck finding a time that will work for everyone when you have more than a few people in the meeting.

Well I *Tried* to Find a Better Time

Years ago when I was the leader of the Fedora Documentation team, we all agreed that our meeting time was bad. At the time, we were a thriving team with a dozen or so regular contributors and even more who helped out around the edges. We had a few Red Hat employees, but most of us (myself included) were volunteer contributors. Team members were in Europe, North America, and Australia (and maybe other continents).

As a responsible and caring team leader, I decided to find a new time that would work better for the team. I set up a survey and shared it in the meeting and on the mailing list. After waiting a week or two, I took a look at the results. The best meeting time was…our current meeting time.

For those who had to stay up very late to attend the meeting, this was a disappointing result. But there wasn't going to be any time that didn't effectively cut off a good chunk of the community. We had to accept it and move on. It's entirely possible that the reason our current time won was that potential contributors who couldn't make the meeting decided not to join the team at all. I have no way of knowing, but that's something to bear in mind.

Some teams hold meetings twice, roughly 12 hours offset give or take, so that people anywhere in the world can attend. Avoid this approach.

The point of meetings is synchronous communication, which you can't have if there are two meetings. Folks who can attend both will feel compelled to do that so they don't miss anything. You've simply doubled the meeting load! At that point, you might as well save everyone the time and put it in an email.

A better approach is to alternate times. If you have a recurring meeting, consider alternating time slots to be globally accessible. For example, you might choose to hold a meeting at noon Eastern time (which is reasonable for Europe, Africa, and the Americas) and midnight Eastern time (which is reasonable for Asia, Oceania, and the Pacific coast of the Americas). This still splits your meeting attendees, but it doesn't duplicate the meeting. With luck, you'll have enough people who can attend both slots to provide some continuity. But at least this way, you've made it so that everyone can attend sometimes, even if no one can attend all the time.

One additional note on scheduling meetings: be aware of the daylight savings time (aka summer). Regardless of your opinions of the concept in general, it's inarguably a pain that not all countries change their clocks at the same time. Among my more useful contributions to the Fedora Project in my time as the Fedora Program Manager have been the twice-yearly "hey, clocks are changing soon! Here's a list of when various countries are changing" emails that I send.

As with time zones, you can't escape daylight savings time; you can only shift the problem. To make the meeting time unambiguous, you could decide to schedule meetings in Coordinated Universal Time (UTC), also known as "Greenwich Mean Time (GMT)" or "Zulu time." The problem with that choice is most people's lives take place in a local time zone, not UTC. This means that the hour that was available for your meeting during the summer might become double-booked during the winter. To avoid this, some teams set meetings for the local time of the person scheduling the meeting. Then it's consistent most of the year, with some confusion for a few weeks in spring and fall. Whichever way you do it, you're deciding which flavor of problem to embrace.

There's a lot to remember in this section, so let's review it quickly. When scheduling a meeting, remember that you're dealing with a global community that participates in different ways. No single meeting time is going to work for everyone. You can address this with alternating—not duplicated—meeting times. Summer time changes happen unevenly, so there will be a few weeks of confusion in the spring and fall. You'll need to accept that your meeting is going to be unworkable for *someone*. You can try to make sure the time works for the key people, but keep in mind what that does for your meeting's inclusivity.

Choose the Medium

Problem: You're not sure what medium to use for a meeting. Text, phone, and video are all options, and these days it seems everyone is on every platform.

The question of how you meet is as important as when you meet. Broadly speaking, you can choose from three categories of meetings: text, phone, and video. Let's take a look at the different options and consider when to use each.

Of course, in-person meetings are also a thing (and they are different enough from video meetings to warrant their own treatment), but they're rare enough in open source projects that we can ignore them for now. Arguably, virtual reality represents another distinct type of meeting. But the only VR meetings I have ever done were social events. I don't see VR meetings becoming common enough to discuss (at least not before the next edition of this book).

Each mode of meeting has strengths and weaknesses. What you pick will, as always, depend on the needs of your project. You may also find that mixing modes works best. In Fedora, most teams conduct text meetings, but the Workstation Working Group and KDE Special Interest Group prefer video meetings. The Fedora Council conducts regular business meetings via text but holds monthly video meetings with guests to look at a particular area of interest within the project.

Text Meetings

For this discussion here, "text meetings" are defined as any typed medium. Some projects use Internet Relay Chat (IRC). Others use Telegram, Matrix, Slack, or whatever else. It doesn't particularly matter for our purposes what platform you use. The right answer is whatever works for your community. You'll learn more about selecting a platform in Appendix 1, Choose Your Tools, on page 149, but for now, let's assume you already have something that works. The following meeting example shows what a text-based meeting looks like.

```
[12:00:00] <bcotton> #startmeeting Example Text Meeting
[12:00:00] <MeetBot> Meeting name set to: example_text_meeting.
[12:00:01] <bcotton> #info This is an example of what a text-based
meeting might look like.
[12:00:03] <bcotton> #info For a reminder of our meeting procedures &
customs, see
[12:00:05] <bcotton> #link https://example.com/MeetingEtiquette
[12:00:10] <bcotton> #topic Roll call
[12:00:30] <alice> good afternoon
[12:00:45] <bob> hey, everyone!
[12:02:00] <bcotton> okay, let's get started
[12:02:10] <bcotton> #topic Old business: Bug 123 - Release 1.0
erases all user data when run on a leap day
[12:02:45] <bcotton> alice: you were going to make sure leap days are
real. have you had a chance to follow up on that?
[12:03:30] <alice> There's a one-in-four chance they are. I think
that's high enough for us to fix this bug
[12:03:45] <alice> #link https://en.wikipedia.org/wiki/February_29
[12:04:15] <bob> yeah, that's bad
[12:04:30] <bcotton> #agreed Leap days are real. We will fix Bug 123
[12:04:35] <bcotton> anything else on this topic?
[12:05:35] <bcotton> #topic New business
[12:05:40] <bcotton> any new business?
[12:05:45] <bob> o/
[12:05:50] <bcotton> go ahead, bob
[12:05:55] <bob> just wanted to show an example of raising my hand
[12:06:00] <bob> all done
[12:06:30] <bcotton> Thanks, bob. Anything else?
[12:07:45] <bcotton> Okay, thanks for coming everyone! See you back
here in two weeks for the next meeting
[12:07:50] <bcotton> #endmeeting
[12:07:50] <MeetBot> Meeting ended logs and minutes are in
https://example.com/meetings/example_text_meeting/
```

You may find the best part of text meetings is that you don't need to put any special effort into note-taking. There's no hurried transcription of what people are saying because they're typing it right out for you. And if you're using something like Debian's MeetBot,[1] you get minutes for free. For example, see the minutes from the following meeting example. It's important that you publish meeting minutes in a place where people will be able to find them. This allows your community to use the minutes as a reference in later conversations and actions. Otherwise, whatever happens in the meeting will be quickly forgotten.

---

1.   https://wiki.debian.org/MeetBot

```
1. a. This is an example of what a text-based meeting might look like.
   b. For a reminder of our meeting procedures & customs, see
   c. https://example.com/MeetingEtiquette

2. Roll call

3. Old business: Bug 123 - Release 1.0 erases all user data when run
on a leap day
   a. https://en.wikipedia.org/wiki/February_29
   b. AGREED: Leap days are real. We will fix Bug 123

4. New business

Meeting ended at 12:07:50 UTC.

Members present:
1. alice
2. bcotton
3. bob
```

Text meetings are also great for your robot friends: search engines. The logs and minutes make it easy for newcomers (and potential newcomers) to learn more about the past of your project. This is a mixed bag, of course. If your project is toxic, then potential contributors will be scared off. If you're worried about that, I suggest putting down this book and fixing that first.

Another great aspect of text meetings is the ability to easily share reference material. Discussing a thorny bug? Share a link. Discussing a glowing review of your latest release? Copy and paste a quote. It's much easier than trying to utter a URL. Think about the video meetings you've been on. Almost all of them have a chat side-channel, right?

Open source project contributors come from all walks of life and all parts of the world. Sometimes this means they're resource-limited. That might mean a lack of bandwidth (including traffic caps), computing hardware, or peripherals. Text-based media tend to be the least resource-intensive, and thus the most inclusive. Consider inclusivity when determining how you'll conduct meetings.

Text meetings also allow people to "multitask." This is a mixed bag, too. Research has shown that people can't multitask, no matter how well they think they can. But it's also the case that meetings don't necessarily require the full attention of all attendees all the time. You may often find yourself lurking in meetings waiting for something to catch your attention. While you're disengaged from the meeting, you can check email, shuffle paperwork, or do other short tasks that allow you to frequently scan what you've missed.

Of course, text meetings aren't perfect. The low-bandwidth nature that makes them the most broadly available also means that you lose a lot of nonverbal communication. The tone of voice doesn't carry well over text (although the increased use of emoji has helped to mitigate that). You also can't read facial expressions the way you could on a video meeting. That has its upsides (you can go get a cup of coffee or play a game on your phone and no one will notice), but that upside is also a downside. In a video call, you can tell when you're losing your audience—to confusion, boredom, or whatever—but in text meetings you can't unless people explicitly tell you (and they often won't).

Text meetings are also slow. Most people talk faster than they type, which means it takes longer to say the same thing in a text meeting. In addition, some platforms don't indicate when someone is typing, so you end up with a lot of pauses to make sure everyone has had their say.

To mitigate this, you have to set a cultural expectation about how text meetings will work. Since it takes a while for a long sentence to be typed, try asking people who want to say something "raise their hand" (by using o/) or type some other short indicator. This becomes increasingly important as the number of attendees grows or the time to cover all the agenda topics shrinks.

For text-based meetings:

- *Have a bot take notes.* It's hard to take notes and participate at the same time. A bot will capture everything with great fidelity and can produce minutes for you as well.

- *Pick a platform approachable by your community.* Your community probably has a chat platform already. Use that.

- *Set expectations about signaling intent to talk.* Many chat platforms don't have a typing indicator, so several people may be typing at once. With an agreed-upon signal to indicate intent to talk, you can call on people in turn. This makes the conversation easier to track.

- *Pause before moving on so that others can type.* As mentioned in the previous point, you may not know if someone is trying to type a message. I like to wait 60 seconds between the time I give a "last call" and setting the new topic.

Video Meetings

In the last few years, video meetings have become an inescapable part of life. This was becoming true before the COVID-19 pandemic and has only accelerated since. As computing power (and bandwidth) has gotten cheaper, video meetings have become a more accessible option.

Video meetings feel more connected than text meetings. You see others' faces and hear their voices. With your clothes, hair, and background, you can share a little of your personality. The participants in a video meeting become people, not just letters on a screen.

You get some direct benefit, too. If you're presenting a proposal, demo, or status update, it's much easier to keep everyone in sync with your slides. If you're whiteboarding, you can talk while you use one of the myriad of shared sketching tools.

Of course, video meetings still require a camera, speakers, microphone, and a reliable broadband Internet. These are a given in much of the world, but you can't necessarily assume your project's contributors will have all of them all of the time. Even if they do, they might not be able to use them (for example, if they're at work or in a shared space).

Running a video meeting probably seems more intuitive to you. It is ultimately a loosely structured conversation and most of us have been having conversations since we were toddlers. It's still important to make sure that the chair calls on the person whose turn it is to speak and that speakers indicate they are done. The video aspect helps you notice when someone is trying to speak up but keeps getting talked over.

For video meetings:

- *Ensure participants have the necessary equipment and bandwidth.* To fully participate in a video meeting, a person needs a webcam. They probably need a headset, especially if they're participating in a place where others are around (like their house). When bandwidth is constrained, shutting off the camera often helps, but that removes much of the benefit of having a video meeting.

- *Separate the duties of leading the meeting and taking notes.* It's difficult to participate in a meeting and take notes at the same time. This is particularly true when you're trying to watch for visual cues from participants, keep an eye on the chat, look at the document under discussion, *and* write notes. Even with a large monitor, that's a lot for your eyes and brain to do at once.

- *Share links to presentations or videos so that participants can follow along on their own.* Screen sharing doesn't always work as well as you want. Some platforms aren't designed for retransmitting a video to many recipients. And some participants may need to increase the text size or use assistive technology.

Phone Meetings

Who loves teleconferences? For the sake of completeness, let's cover phone meetings in brief. Let's define "phone" as a spoken medium without video. It may be a traditional telephone service or an Internet-based service like Skype. Phone meetings are an unhappy medium between text and video. People get talked over without any way of trying to indicate who wants to talk. Referring to URLs and visual elements like slides is nigh impossible. Participants who don't speak the same native language may have trouble understanding each other. You don't get the benefits of either of those media (other than the tone of voice). They're not very inclusive unless the service you use has a toll-free number for each country your participants are from. For these reasons, I'm not aware of any open source project that uses phone meetings as a primary form of communication.

But you may find phone calls become more appealing for one-on-one conversations. The phrase "Zoom fatigue" entered our vocabulary during the COVID-19 pandemic as more people began living their entire lives in video conferences. You feel drained after performing for the camera all day, and many people discovered they preferred a phone call instead of a video call. If you're talking to one other person and want to do it over the phone, go for it.

For phone meetings:

- *Ensure the platform has toll-free dial-in numbers for all participants.* In most cases, toll-free numbers are specific to a country. This means if you have a participant from a country where the platform doesn't have a number, they'll have to pay to dial in. International calling isn't cheap.

- *Ask participants to identify themselves every time they speak.* You probably don't know everyone's voice, even if you've been in the project for many years. If everyone identifies themselves, it's always clear who is talking.

- *Call on participants in turn to prevent cross-talk.* When multiple people on a conference call are talking at the same time, it's impossible to understand any of them. As the moderator, you have to call on people when it is their turn to talk. The challenge here is that the only way people can let you know they want to talk is by talking.

Make Your Meeting Productive

Problem: Your meetings feel like a waste of time. People are skipping them more often.

Meetings have a bad reputation because many of them are poorly run. People don't mind productive meetings, so let's see how we can make meetings useful.

It's not enough to simply hold a meeting; you've been to plenty of aimless meetings, adrift on a sea of poor planning. A productive meeting requires planning. This is especially important in open source projects. Unlike in an unproductive corporate meeting where everyone is getting paid to be there, an unproductive community meeting is a waste of the precious time that your contributors donate to you.

To hold a productive meeting, you have to do work before, during, and after the meeting. The work starts with preparing and communicating an agenda. Then you have to run the meeting itself. Finally, you have to document and share the outcome of the meeting.

Prepare the Meeting Agenda

Problem: Nobody knows what the meeting will cover when they show up. They don't know if it'll be relevant to them or if there's any prework they should do to prepare.

Every meeting needs an agenda. The ideal agenda includes the topics that'll be covered, links to reference materials, and the desired outcome. Most meeting agendas fall short of the ideal, but if you can at least get close, that helps. Even if a meeting is a regular event, you need to indicate why that particular instance is important. For example, if the meeting is to review open bugs, list the particular bugs to be discussed.

Why have an agenda? First, it gives your attendees time to prepare. If they need to review the history of a bug or read a proposal draft to have an informed discussion, they can do that before the meeting instead of during it. Second, it gives your attendees the opportunity to decide they don't need to be present. If they have nothing to contribute and don't particularly care about the outcome, they might decide there are better uses of their time. In fact, some people will reject on principle any invitations that don't include an agenda.

The previous paragraph implies an additional action: sharing the agenda. As a bonus, this helps remind people that the meeting is going to happen. The point is to give people some time to read the agenda and prepare.

For recurring meetings, a good goal is sending the agenda a day in advance. Try to aim for the 24-hour mark, even if it generally ends up closer to 20-ish. Sending the agenda an hour or two before the meeting is a lot less helpful. People in another time zone might not wake up until right before the meeting.

Others might be in another meeting before yours. 24 hours is a reasonable balance between giving attendees time to prepare and the risk of the topics becoming stale before the meeting happens.

For one-off meetings, have the agenda ready before you send invitations. This allows people to immediately decide if the meeting is worth their time. Remember the people that reject agendaless meeting invitations? If a full agenda isn't possible, provide as much of the agenda as you can. Give your attendees a clear expectation of when they can expect the final agenda. The more reading, thinking, or other premeeting homework attendees need to do, the more advance notice you should give them.

To prepare a good agenda:

- *Include links to supporting material like proposals under consideration or bugs to triage.* If you give attendees the opportunity to "do their homework" in advance, everyone can come to the meeting prepared.

- *Share the agenda at least a day in advance.* This gives people a chance to decide if the meeting is relevant to them and to do any prep work if it is.

- *Allow late additions for discussion only.* When you set the expectation that people should skip meetings that aren't valuable, you have to expect that they will. If you add a topic at the last minute and then vote on it, you're excluding people who can't attend or decided not to.

- *Specify the expected outcomes for the meeting.* This lets everyone know what the meeting is supposed to accomplish, which helps you keep the meeting on track.

Chair the Meeting

Problem: The meeting is chaotic. Participants are speaking over each other and jumping from topic to topic.

A good chair keeps the meeting on track. Like a conductor leading an orchestra, the chair guides the group to keep them in sync. The meeting flows from topic to topic and everyone can be heard in turn.

Chairing a meeting is more art than science. There's no algorithm to running a perfect meeting. Meetings are a reflection of the organization's culture, too, so what works in one group might be oppressively formal in another. With time and practice, you'll come to learn what works best for you and your project.

This general flow works well as a starting point for most meetings:

1. *Take roll.* For text meetings, have people say a brief hello to indicate they are present. For video meetings, take note of who is on the call. Unless the point of the meeting is to make introductions, don't use up your valuable time by having everyone introduce themselves.

2. *State the meeting's purpose and process.* Don't spend too much time on this. Give a sentence or two explaining what the meeting is, plus any special procedures used in the meeting (for example, how to signal intent to talk). If you have a shared note-taking document, remind everyone to use it.

3. *Review the previous meeting's action items.* Start with a review of what was supposed to be done. If tasks remain open, leave them on the list for the next meeting. If a task has been stalled for a while, reassign it or abandon it. Of course, this only applies when there's a previous meeting to refer back to.

4. *Address the topics on the agenda.* Begin with the most important and time-sensitive topics and work down the list to the least important. That way, if you run out of time, you've at least covered the pressing issues.

5. *Open the floor for additional discussion.* If there's time, you can discuss (but not decide) issues that weren't on the agenda or revisit anything that was tabled earlier in the meeting. If the meeting's chair rotates, assign the next meeting's chair before moving to open floor.

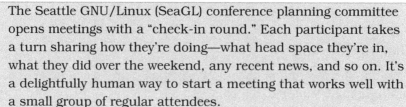

An Exception to the "No Introductions" Rule

The Seattle GNU/Linux (SeaGL) conference planning committee opens meetings with a "check-in round." Each participant takes a turn sharing how they're doing—what head space they're in, what they did over the weekend, any recent news, and so on. It's a delightfully human way to start a meeting that works well with a small group of regular attendees.

Notice that reviewing the previous meeting's action items comes early in the flow. This is important, even when the result of the action item is a topic later in the agenda. In general, you want to start with "old business" first. This way, if you run out of time, you still had the follow-up. If you don't cover old business first and several consecutive meetings run late, you may find that the old business never gets resolved. What happens is that more new business piles on top of the old. Of course, if an agenda topic is time-critical (like if it must be discussed before the next meeting comes around), it's okay to break the guidelines and put it first.

For years, I was a net control operator for my local Amateur Radio Emergency Services group. Severe weather is a regular threat in my part of the world, so we had plenty of opportunities to develop our skills. This practice has carried over pretty well to managing meetings—text meetings in particular.

These are a few tips that will serve you well:

- *Be as succinct as possible (but no more).* When you have to type everything out, time is a precious commodity. Try to get your message across as clearly and directly as possible. Don't repeat yourself.

- *Clearly indicate to whom you're talking.* If you're asking a specific person a question or responding to them, say their name or chat handle at the beginning of the message.

- *Have people signal that they want to talk and indicate whose turn it is.* If you let it be a free-for-all, you might end up with five people starting five different threads at once. In text meetings, you might have an agreed indication, such as a raised hand (by using o/) or a single punctuation mark. Many video chat platforms have a "raise hand" function.

- *Indicate when you're done talking.* If you're sending a multiline message, it's not always obvious when you're done. So say that you are. If the attendees are programmers, "EOF" is an easy way to express that.

- *Have a script.* Following a script helps administrivia become routine. It also helps participants become accustomed to how the meetings operate.

- *Remember that you're in charge.* A meeting is not the time for power tripping, but as the chair, you're there to facilitate communication. That means stepping in and moving the conversation along when it gets out of control.

- *Stop people when they're off-topic.* It's okay to stop the conversation when it gets too far afield. You can come back to it at the end or ask folks to take it to a different venue.

- *Know when to relax—and when to be more strict.* On the other hand, it's okay to be a little more relaxed with the meeting rules. If the agenda is light, the conversation is productive, and the matter isn't urgent, you can let things go a bit. If the meeting is an incident response chat, it's probably better to keep the jokes in another channel. If the topic is contentious and people are getting chippy, you may want to go to more formal speaking rules to keep a fight from breaking out.

Follow up After the Meeting

Problem: Your meetings are productive, but nothing happens afterward. Action items remain undone.

Bad news! Your work isn't done when the meeting ends. You have tasks to complete postmeeting. These tasks make sure the decisions and assignments that happened in your productive meeting don't get lost in the great cosmic void.

For example, you might need to go back and fill in details for the minutes and then post those to the place where your project shares meeting minutes. You need to create or update the tickets in your project's tracker. (If your project doesn't already have a ticket tracker, see the section Ticket Tracker, on page 158.) You might need to schedule a follow-up meeting. As a rough approximation, plan on pre- and post-meeting work taking about half the amount of time the meeting does.

Make Decisions in the Right Place

Problem: Community members are excluded from decisions. They feel unvalued and you miss out on important input.

I've alluded to this in a few places already, but I want to say it very directly before the chapter comes to an end: where you make your decisions matters. You may wonder why I essentially repeated the title of the section in the very first sentence. Because it's important, that's why. I talked about this in Take a Vote, on page 39, but it can't be said often enough.

If you're only making decisions in meetings, you're severely restricting who can be a part of the decision-making process. This is particularly true if you allow in-meeting additions to the agenda. Issues can arise even when everyone is in the same building. Sit back and relax, because I am going to share an illustrative story.

What's in a Name?

Many years and several jobs ago, my team had a weekly change approval board meeting. If you wanted to make a significant change to the research computing infrastructure, particularly anything that might impact the users, you brought it to this meeting. This gave team members who were experts in other systems a chance to say "uh, no, you'll break this other thing" and it gave the user support folks a heads-up.

When I first joined the team, everyone went to this meeting every week. Our manager wisely realized that this wasn't a great use of our time, so he made a point of telling us that we should feel free to skip it if we didn't have anything we wanted to discuss. To make that possible, he shared the agenda ahead of time. Don't see anything you care about? Don't go!

This worked pretty well, until one fateful day when it very much did not. At the end of the meeting, one of the team leads brought up the need to rename a cluster. You see, we had a small cluster of old hardware that was a test bed for us systems folks. The new research cluster that we were bringing up later that year had just been named by the CIO and he happened to pick the name of the professor for whom the test cluster was named. We'll say that's "Jones" for the purpose of this story. Prior to the CIO naming the future cluster, we had been calling it "Sprinkles." So now that the new cluster was going to be called "Jones," what should we rename the old cluster? A team lead proposed "Sprinkles" and that name was accepted.

When the notes from the meeting were shared, my office mate and I were upset. We went to both of the team leads and the manager, expressing our concerns about the name that was chosen and more importantly, the fact that it was done without being on the agenda. Had we known that decision was coming, we'd have attended the meeting and objected. The next few months vindicated us as the team had to constantly disambiguate not one but two clusters. "Do you mean New Sprinkles or Old Sprinkles?" and "Do you mean New Jones or Old Jones?" were common questions among our staff.

By breaking the process, the team got saddled with a funny-in-the-moment-but-actually-super-obnoxious-for-months-to-come decision. The agenda's credibility was damaged, and several of us returned to attending every meeting just in case.

For open source projects, the effects of last-minute decisions in meetings can be worse than silly name choices. Instead, you're excluding members of your community from the process. Contributors who don't feel like they have a voice will often find other projects. In general, you should make decisions asynchronously. When you must make a decision in a meeting, try to wait until you've allowed time for open discussion first.

Retrospective

Meetings are a challenge in global, community-driven projects, but they provide a lot of value to your community when done well. To have an effective meeting, you need to plan it well. Schedule it at a time that maximizes participation on a platform that doesn't exclude contributors. Develop an agenda in advance (and cancel the meeting if you don't have one!). Run the meeting with an eye toward making sure everyone understands the process and has an opportunity to participate. And, finally, follow up after the meeting to share the notes and any action items.

If that sounds like a lot of work, it is. But the work you put into meetings will directly impact what your community gets out of them.

## CHAPTER 7

Develop Your Release Life Cycle

To plan the schedule and features that you'll do in the next two chapters, you need to decide on the life cycle of the release. You need to know how frequently you'll release, how many releases you'll work on at once, and how long until you stop working on them. Given infinite resources, you'd support every release forever. In reality, you need to balance long-term support with new development. As usual, there's no one-size-fits-all approach, so let's take a look at your options.

Decide How Many

Problem: You need to decide how many parallel releases to support.

The first question you ask yourself when determining a release life cycle isn't "how long?" but "how many?" The simplest form of a release life cycle is a single continuous stream, updated repeatedly forever (or until you abandon the project). You publish a release and people use it until the next release comes out.

This is simple because the only supported version is the latest version. But it also requires that upgrades are trivial for users to perform and never fail or change existing behavior. And it locks developers into decisions that were made early on. You can do a total rewrite and drop that into place, but if it changes existing behavior, you'll alienate some of your users.

The "we only have one active release ever" model can work for projects with small developer teams and no downstreams. It might not be ideal, but it's a reasonable reality for an under-resourced volunteer project. Larger projects, particularly complex ones or ones with downstreams, need to consider how many parallel releases will exist. Even if you're only developing one at a time, you'll want to have some overlap in supported releases to give users time to move to the new version. Counterintuitively, the more development work you'll do in the next release (in terms of the scope and impact of the changes), the more development work you will need to have done on the previous release. The more significant the changes are for users, the longer it'll take them to upgrade to the new release, so they will expect smaller features to continue to be added to the older version.

Let's get meta for a moment and use this book as an example. Before publication, it went through a beta phase with several releases. Each beta release was (more or less) a new chapter. So I worked on one chapter at a time. If I had ideas for what to write in other chapters, I put them in a notes file and focused on my one in-development release. But, because I was getting feedback from the beta readers, I also made changes to previously written chapters. Even though I was writing new and exciting content, readers still needed me to fix "bugs" in previous releases. Of course, this analogy is imperfect (as all analogies are), but it illustrates the point.

Having only one release in development at a time makes the most sense, with a caveat: "development" can have different meanings. As you'll see in the next section, you may still be doing development after shipping a release. So as we think about "how many?" here, let's think about significant releases. Having only one significant release in development at a time makes the most sense. The main exception is if you're working on a total redesign, in which case you might have some of your developers focused on the brand-new version while others work on interim releases. Realistically, most open source projects don't have the number of contributors (and multiyear planning) to make this an option.

So we're set on having one development release at a time. How many supported releases should you have? The answer depends on how much your community can support and how your users use the software. Adding more supported releases increases the demands on your community. It takes more effort from developers and testers—backporting bug fixes to older versions becomes increasingly difficult over time. It also requires more technical resources: storage, build farms, and so on. If your software is the end goal (a web browser, for example), you can have fewer supported releases in parallel. But if your software is a building block for other things (like an operating system or programming language), you may need several releases. In general, you can start with one supported previous release at a time for "end" projects. For "building block" projects, you'll want to support at least two previous releases, and at least one from the last compatibility change (for example, Python 2.7 was supported long after Python 3 was ready for general use).

You Can Only Change Your Life Cycle in One Direction

It's best to be conservative—or pessimistic—when setting your initial life cycle. Plan for it to take more effort and technical resources than you reasonably expect. Once you have some real-world experience with the project, you can add more concurrently supported versions. Your users will appreciate the pleasant surprise. If you reduce the number of supported versions unexpectedly, your users will resent the unpleasant surprise. It'll damage your project's reputation, even if the reason makes sense. Always aim to underpromise and overdeliver.

Set the Phases

Problem: You need to decide what level of support to provide.

The first thing that comes to mind when you think of a "life cycle" is probably a set of phases. Humans start out as infants and then become toddlers. Eventually, they turn into teenagers and adults. Like humans, software also goes through phases. In each phase, a different level of support is required, and there are different expectations. Let's not abuse the metaphor by trying to directly map software to humans, but the first question to ask when setting the life cycle is "what phases do we have?"

In the remainder of this section, we'll look at different phases you might include in your release life cycle. Most of them are optional. In fact, the simplest model is to have a continuous release where you only support the current state of the code repository. But most projects will have some kind of release model. Which phases you choose to include will depend on the kind of software you're developing, the use case you want to support, and the resources you have to provide support for each phase.

Before we look at the phases, let's come to a common understanding of releases. Semantic Versioning[1] (SemVer) is a standard for versioning software based on the characteristics of the changes in the new version. In brief, software has a version number of X.Y.Z, where X (the "major version") is incremented when you introduce backwards-incompatible changes, Y (the "minor version") is incremented when you introduce compatible changes, and Z (the "patch version") is incremented when you make bug fixes that don't change the public API. Not every project uses SemVer, but it gives us a useful mental model to think about releases. When we discuss a "release" in the rest of this section, let's think of it as a "major release." (Although if your project rarely

---

1.   https://semver.org/

makes incompatible changes, it may make more sense to shift the definition of release to "minor release" in the SemVer sense.)

Development

The first phase is development. It's not optional: this is where you're designing and writing the software. You haven't formally released it yet, but it might be available to adventurous users. In this phase, the software is unsupported in the sense that you don't necessarily expect it to work for end-user use cases. But you'll fix bugs because that's part of development. Users should expect the software to be buggy or incomplete in this phase because you're still in the middle of writing it. There are two release milestones that you want to consider as part of the development phase: alpha and beta.

An alpha release is designed to give users an early look at what's coming next in your software. Alphas are expected to be buggy and incomplete. They're more about showing the general direction of features and less about the exact experience. Features are minimally complete—or sometimes incomplete—for an alpha release.

Alpha releases are hardly universal and have become less common with time. Before easy access to source repositories existed, an alpha release made a lot of sense. Nowadays, you can get the benefits of an alpha release by pointing curious users to the tip of the development branch or your CI builds. For "foundational" projects (programming languages, enterprise operating systems, or major frameworks), the formality of an alpha release is a good way to get feedback on the general design of your next release. For most projects, it's probably an unnecessary effort.

Beta releases are intended to get feedback from your most engaged users in production-like settings. The code should be mostly complete. You might have some additional polishing or performance improvements to do, but the functionality should all be there. Many open source projects do a beta release to widen the scope of testing beyond the core QA team. If you have downstream projects, the beta release is also a sign to them they should start preparing.

Active Support

Shipping the release doesn't mean you're done with it. There are still bugs to fix and maybe some features to add. Unless you go with a "we only have one release ever" model, a release is only the beginning.

In the active support phase, work can seem similar to the development phase. In addition to fixing bugs, projects often add smaller features. You wouldn't make incompatible changes or significantly update the user interface, but you might add new functionality that didn't exist before. For example, if you're making a text editor, you might add syntax support for a new programming language. You might also add support for a new platform—either a hardware architecture or an operating system—in the active support phase, provided that it doesn't require backwards-incompatible changes. This phase is where you'd make what Semantic Versioning calls "minor releases."

"Support" is a loaded term—not everyone shares a definition. Some people think it means they can ask you a question and you'll help them until they get an answer. Unless you're charging money, that's probably not what you mean. More likely, you mean something like "we'll make a best-effort attempt to fix the bugs that we can and maybe backport some new features from the next release." That's fine, so long as you communicate it clearly. You get to define what "support" means for you.

Maintenance

After support comes the maintenance phase. This is essentially a pared-down version of support. In the maintenance phase, you're not going to add any new features, but you'll still fix bugs. You might choose to limit the bugs you fix. Perhaps you'll ignore cosmetic bugs but fix bugs that cause crashes. In this phase, you're generally only going to make what Semantic Versioning calls "patch releases."

Some projects skip the active support phase and jump straight to maintenance. Others will stop after active support (or skip ahead to the security phase). The only right way is the one that works for you. In addition to your resources, which approach you pick will also depend on what kind of software you're producing and who uses it. For end-user software that gets updates from a built-in mechanism or a distribution repository, it might not matter as much. People will be running the latest software regardless. In that case, you might end at the active support phase. But for enterprise applications, programming languages, and other things where the user wants some long-term stability, they'll expect to have a maintenance period, even if it means there's a short or nonexistent active support period.

Security

The security phase is a subset of the maintenance phase. Whereas in maintenance you might fix any (or most) bugs, in the security phase you're only going to fix security bugs. You might not even worry about all security bugs, only the most critical ones. Again, you can draw the line however you choose, but you need to make expectations clear up front. Like in the maintenance phase, you're primarily making "patch releases."

As with the other phases, you're not obligated to have a security phase. Cynically, the security phase is "people are using this release longer than we want them to, but we figure it's better for everyone if we don't leave security holes unfixed." But no one can reasonably expect you to fix old software forever. Eventually, even the security phase comes to an end.

Long-Term Support

Long-term support (LTS) isn't a separate phase so much as it is a deviation from the usual. It extends a support phase—or phases—longer than normal. Adding long-term support to the occasional release is a good way to balance the stability needs of your users with the demands a longer support cycle places on your developers.

When might you choose to make your project an LTS release? Well, if you want to, for one. Or if your users ask for it. But users will ask for a lot, so you don't have to do it because someone asks. In general, if your project is something that others build on, you should consider having an LTS release. Programming languages, frameworks, and enterprise operating systems are all obvious candidates. In general, the bigger the differences between your releases, the more strongly you should consider having an occasional LTS release. The more work your downstream users will have to do to migrate to a new version, the more likely they are to want something they can rely on for a long time.

If you've decided to have LTS releases, the next question is "which releases?" You can't make every release an LTS release because then none of them are—you just have a long support cycle. Some projects have predictable LTS releases. Ubuntu, for example, makes every fourth release an LTS. Since there's an Ubuntu release twice a year, you can count on an LTS release every two years. On the other hand, the Linux kernel chooses an LTS release based on "major new features, popular commercial distribution needs, device manufacturer demand, maintainer workload and availability,"[2] and other factors. While in recent years, this has worked out to an LTS roughly every 12 months, it's not set in stone. In 2014 alone, the Linux kernel had three LTS releases.

If your release schedule is predictable and the amount of change between releases is roughly equal, setting a regular pattern for LTS releases is the

---

2. https://www.kernel.org/category/releases.html#what-is-the-next-longterm-release-going-to-be

right way to go. This gives your developers and your users clear expectations ahead of time. If either the schedule or the feature set varies wildly, go for an ad hoc approach. Offer a smaller release for one or two releases after the majorly disruptive one so people have had time to adjust to the big changes.

Set the Length

Problem: You need to decide how long each of the support phases lasts.

Now that you've determined how many releases you'll support and to what level, it's time to figure out how long each phase lasts. To do that, you'll need to understand your users and your contributor community. There's a certain minimum time where, if you don't support a release for at least that long, your users will get mad and go find another software package to do the job for them. You want to go past that minimum.

Of course, each person has their own particular minimum, but in general, it comes down to how difficult the upgrade process is. That's more than just the process of acquiring and installing the new bits. Changes in the UI and workflow increase the difficulty. Even when the changes are inarguably for the better, the cognitive effort of learning the new way presents a barrier to the user. The pain is magnified when changes break how other software interacts with yours. If your update breaks the user's plugins or causes their scripts to fail, the minimum length gets much longer.

"Support" here can be any combination of the active, maintenance, and security phases in the previous section. If you have more than one phase, you'll probably want to divide them roughly evenly. For example, having 11 months of active support and one month of maintenance support is unnecessarily complex. Simply offer six months of active support and six months of maintenance support or a year of either.

A good starting point is to set the support period to be the length of the development period times the number of concurrently supported releases. If you decided to have two supported releases and each release is developed over a six-month period, then you'd support each release for a year. With three supported releases and a one-year development cycle, each release is supported for three years. You'll want to add on a little bit extra at the end to give users some overlap if they want to skip versions. A good rule of thumb is to add the same number of the next smaller units of time. For example, if you plan for a six-month support period, add six weeks of overlap with the latest release. If you have a one-year support period, add an extra month to the end. This rule of thumb gets less useful toward the extremes, but it's a good starting point for the one-to-five-year range.

Of course, you can always take these guidelines and extend them. Nothing can stop you from offering a century of support for each release. But reality will probably make a liar out of you. As with the number of supported releases, you want to start out conservatively. You can extend the support period later if you have the need and ability. As you read in the warning on page 73, you'll do reputational harm to your project if you shorten the support period after release.

Retrospective

Now that you've set your release life cycle, you can start planning the release. You know how many releases you're supporting in parallel, what kind of support they receive, and for how long. This helps your community know where to put the effort in the development cycle. It's also important for your users and downstream projects so they can plan appropriately. If you're still trying to figure out what works best for your project, endoflife.date[3] makes it easy to look at the life cycles of various open source and proprietary projects. You can compare your project to your peers' projects and see what works for them. But for now, let's start working on your release schedule.

---

3.   https://endoflife.date/

## CHAPTER 8

Build a Release Schedule

In the previous chapter, you set the release's life cycle. Now it's time to plan how to make the release a reality. The release schedule is the most important document you'll produce as a program manager. It represents the project's *plan of record*—the agreed-upon listing of who will do what and when they'll do it. Your community will rely on it to know what's coming up and use it to measure progress.

Even if it's obvious to you that you need to have a schedule, it's still worth examining the different reasons. How you build, track, and modify your schedule will vary with the relative importance of each reason. If you think you don't need a schedule, you may be right. Still, you may want a "schedule" that doesn't have specific dates attached to track the overall development flow and any dependencies. Think of it like a progress bar: even if you don't actually know where the end is, it's helpful to know if you're 25% or 75% of the way there.

A Schedule's Purpose

Problem: The community doesn't understand why you need a schedule. They ask "can't we ship when it's done?"

So why have a schedule? Most importantly, it helps you coordinate the release. The larger and more organized your project's community, the more important this becomes. You have teams depending on the output of other teams, so you need agreement on when those dependencies will be met. Think about it: how can you deliver your work on time to the people who depend on it if you don't know when they need it? Some tasks may take a while, and you probably don't want to start them the night before the release. And, if we're being honest with each other, a schedule helps you figure out when you're done. Rare is the software that is truly considered complete; there are always more features to add and bugs to fix.

Your project's schedule is also important to your users. Not all users care, of course. Some stay on their first version forever. Others upgrade through whatever automatic mechanism is available and never think about it. But your highly engaged users do care. They're the ones who are interested in your road map and look forward to whatever cool new feature you have planned for the next release. If you keep these users informed and engaged, you get word-of-mouth publicity and maybe even convert some of them into contributors.

If you have downstream projects, they care, too. Whether your project is a library that is used in user-facing projects or an application that is shipped in a distribution, downstreams don't like surprises. If you have a schedule, your downstreams can know if a new version is about to come out. They may choose to adjust their release date to make sure they can bring in the latest version. Or else they'll at least know that major changes are landing and be prepared for extra testing.

Conversely, you also care about your downstreams' schedules. For example, the GNOME Project generally releases new versions each March and September. This works out well because two of their major downstreams—Ubuntu and Fedora Linux—happen to release in April and October. By releasing ahead of the distros, GNOME gets the new version into the hands of users quickly. Similarly, when Python adopted PEP 602[1] to switch to an annual release cycle, one of the reasons was that it

> allows for synchronizing the schedule of Python release management with external
> distributors like Fedora who've been historically very helpful in finding regressions
> early not only in core Python but also in third-party libraries.

If you flip the GNOME and Python examples around, you can see that upstream projects will sometimes care about your schedule, too. This is particularly true when your project is a distribution or another integrator since that's how many users get their software these days. Your upstreams want to make sure that your users can start using the upstream software as soon as possible, so they may want to align with your schedule. Of course, you're not the only upstream for most of your downstreams, so most of them probably don't care too much about your schedule in practice—or at least can't get closer to yours without getting out of alignment with another. But even if they

---

1. https://www.python.org/dev/peps/pep-0602/

can't align themselves to your schedule, they can make informed decisions based on it.

Choose a Schedule Model

Problem: You don't know if your schedule should target a specific date or the completion of an agreed set of work.

No two project schedules are alike, but most of them will fall into one of three basic categories: calendar-based, feature-based, and whim-based. Let's examine the last one first; it's very simple and then we can put it aside for the rest of the chapter.

"Whim-based" schedules aren't actually schedules: you're deciding to release on a whim. In most cases, you're probably not going to wake up one morning and say "I think today is release day!" What probably happens is that you have some time to get some work done on the project and you say "okay, that's it for now."

Whim-based schedules are fine for projects with a solo developer and a small user base. As you add more contributors and a larger user community, you'll probably want to have at least a minimally structured schedule for coordination purposes.

So let's return to the two real schedule models! Calendar-based schedules are what they sound like: you pick a day on the calendar that you want to ship your release and build a schedule back from that date. Feature-based schedules go the other direction. Start with a list of the features you want to add (and perhaps the bugs you want to fix) and work forward. Obviously, the calendar-based schedule's planned release date will be more firm than the feature-based one. But the resulting schedules will generally look fairly similar in structure.

Or No Schedule

If your project does continuous delivery or a rolling release, you're not going to have a schedule. The concepts in this chapter still apply. If you think about each individual feature as its own release, then you can take some of the milestones discussed later in the chapter and use them as gates. Just as you wouldn't merge the feature until the code tests pass, you can block the merge until the appropriate documentation is written and changed strings are translated.

No right choice exists for the schedule model—it depends on the needs and preferences of your community. In general, though, the larger (particularly in terms of user base or influence in the broader ecosystem) your project becomes, the more you should lean toward a calendar-based schedule. The predictability a calendar-based schedule provides to upstreams, downstreams, and users outweighs the developer flexibility of a feature-based schedule.

Feature-based schedules are a better fit for projects where all of the development work is related. If everyone is working on different parts of the same software (a web browser or container engine, for example), the inherently Agile nature of a feature-based schedule makes sense. If your project is aggregating or integrating many upstream projects (like a Linux distribution), then you'll find the firm deadlines of a calendar-based approach much easier to work with. But be careful: feature-based schedules have a tendency to slip indefinitely. How long were we waiting for "Duke Nukem Forever?"[2]

Define "Done"

Problem: The community doesn't have a shared view of the release target.

When do you know that your release is done? We need to come to a common definition. For a calendar-based schedule, this is the planned release date. For a feature-based schedule, this is the planned feature set. Next, we'll explore these two definitions.

Calendar-Based Schedule

Problem: You've decided to go with a calendar-based schedule, but you're not sure which date to pick for the release target.

Look at the calendar. Pick a date. Done!

Okay, it's not that simple. But we can come up with a suitable target date. The first thing you want to do is to make sure that your planned date is far enough out to actually get the work done. How long will it take you to get the work done if you put this book down right now and get to work?

Picking a date in the past is obviously a nonstarter unless you have a time machine (can I borrow it?). Picking a date in the next month is probably not great for most projects of any significant size. There's a bit of a circular dependency here: you don't know how long it will take to do the work until you have done it a few times, but you can't do the work until you have developed a schedule. (Well, unless you're currently using a feature-based or

---

2. https://en.wikipedia.org/wiki/Duke_Nukem_Forever

a whim-based schedule, but switching schedule models will affect how you approach the work, so even then it's only a rough estimate.)

Despite the fact we're calling this model "calendar-based," there's an element of feature consideration at play. You want releases to be "different enough." The definition of this term is context-dependent: what's different enough for a web browser is probably not different enough for an operating system. Also, you pay an "effort cost" in doing the release, and your users pay a "cognitive cost" in determining whether the impact of an upgrade is worth their effort. Enterprise operating systems and programming languages tend to have schedules measured in years because any faster is too much for users to keep up with. Desktop environments and hobbyist operating systems can work well with half a year. User applications can look at schedules as short as a month.

With all of this in mind, you can roughly approximate what value of "too soon" applies to your project. You're probably using the software your community produces. How often do you want to upgrade?

Now that you know what's out of bounds, it's time to pick an actual release date. So how do you do that?

Start with anything that naturally presents a deadline. For example, if you're giving a talk at a conference, you'll probably want to make sure the release is out by the time you get on stage. Saying "and you can try it out now in our latest release!" sounds much better than "it will be out soon." You can also look at the schedules of important upstream and downstream projects. Are you expecting users to run your application with Python 3.10? Then you probably don't want to release before Python 3.10 is out. Similarly, if you'd like your latest update to ship in the next version of your favorite Linux distribution, you need to ship before the deadline for that distro's package updates.

Picking a release date doesn't have to be serious business. Some dates are just fun. For example, a project for the Raspberry Pi could pick March 14—Pi Day—as a release date. On the other hand, you might want to *avoid* Pi Day so that your release doesn't get lost in the deluge of Pi Day stories.

You could also pick a date based on tradition. If your project has generally released in February, pick a day in February. Or pick your pet's birthday. As long as you pick a date, you've done your job. Now let's work backward to add in the necessary schedule milestones.

Not All Dates Are Equal

When picking a target date, consider what happens if the schedule slips. Planning your release for the week before Christmas leads to a Christmas Day release if you have to delay by a week. Your community may not appreciate being asked to spend a holiday getting the release out the door.

Similarly, public perception matters, too. The Fedora Linux release schedule intentionally targets the third Tuesday of April and October. This means a one-week adjustment—which is common since the early target is optimistic—is still in the same month. The difference between April 20 and April 27 is the same as the difference between April 27 and May 4 in terms of the number of days, but the fact that one date is in April and the other in May makes the latter feel like a bigger slip.

When you build a calendar-based schedule, you may choose to repeat it. You can copy version 1.0's schedule, update the release date, and call it version 2.0's schedule. This has the benefit of being predictable for your contributors and users and gives them a chance to plan a release or two in advance. Of course, the future schedules will probably need adjustment over time as your project's needs change (or you discover glaring inaccuracies in your schedule).

If you're starting a project from scratch, it might take a few tries before you get into a predictable release cadence, and that's okay. You don't need to start repeating the schedule before you can reasonably meet it. The choices you make about your project's life cycle in *Develop Your Release Life Cycle* will impact how repeatable your schedule can be.

Feature-Based Schedules

Problem: You picked a feature-based schedule, but you don't know how to scope the size of the release.

Feature-based schedules work in the opposite direction from their calendar-based counterparts. To build out a feature-based schedule, you start with building a list of features to include in the release. Then you layer on the subsequent steps. So how do you build your list of targeted features?

Well, how different do you want the new release to be? If you pick too small of a set, you run the risk of releasing too often and overloading your users' brains with frequent "do I need this update and what happens if I take it?"

questions. You also cause your community to spend a lot of time on release notes, website updates, marketing, and other activities tied to a release. And if you rely on reviews on popular websites or tech publications to help drive interest, you will find that too frequent releases result in white noise rather than buzz.

On the other hand, if you make it too large, it's going to take reviewers and users a lot of time to figure out everything that changed and what to do about it. If you introduce too much incompatibility (or what the users perceive as incompatibility), the cost of switching to another project gets close to the cost of switching to your latest version. Of course, sometimes you can't help but introduce incompatibilities. When you have several incompatible features, it's better to bundle them into one release instead of adding a new compatibility-breaker with every release. That's a good recipe for driving away users.

Another good case for bundling is when you have interdependent features. Two features that are entirely unrelated don't need to go in the same release. On the other hand, if the new remote control feature requires Bluetooth to work, you'll want to make sure you include Bluetooth support with (or before) the release with the remote control feature.

Despite the "feature-based schedule" name, the calendar is inescapable. Another consideration for sizing your feature set is how long you want the release to take. It's okay if the date isn't entirely predictable—picking a target quarter is fine. The point is that you don't want it to drag on for several years. Going five years between releases will cause a lot of people to assume your project is dead.

Once you have a solid feature set defined, you're ready to add in the rest of your schedule.

Add Milestones

Problem: You have a release target set, but you don't know what steps it takes to get there.

After you have defined "done," the act of building the schedule is largely the same: picking the milestones you want and how far before the release day they should fall. In this section, we'll look at some key milestones to add to the schedule. The true value of the schedule is in the steps that build up to the end date and the dependencies between those steps. The schedule tells your community what they need to do and the degree to which the deadlines are met on time tells you how the release is going.

Milestones Versus Tasks

A *milestone* is a point-in-time marker that you can use to see how far along you are. Like a signpost on the highway, it's an instantaneous measure. On your schedule, a milestone has a duration of zero—it starts and ends at the same time. A *task*, on the other hand, is a thing that people do. It may take a few minutes or a few weeks. Your schedule will likely contain a mix of tasks and milestones.

Teams can't follow a schedule unless they see themselves in it. This means that your schedule has to include more than the "core" release milestones. You have to involve the rest of the community. Whether you have formalized teams or particular individuals who perform roles, part of developing your schedule involves sitting down with them. You need to know what they plan on doing, when they plan on doing it, and what they depend on from others in order to do it.

As you add milestones to your schedule, think about the dependencies. Which tasks must be completed before the milestone? Which must be started? What tasks depend on other tasks?

The remainder of this section discusses some possible milestones you can consider. What you pick depends on the type and scale of your project, as well as the choices you made in *Develop Your Release Life Cycle*. I have grouped some of these milestones by functional area, which may or may not match how your project is structured. Most importantly, don't take this section as exhaustive. You'll come up with many other tasks to fill in. Think about what you'd add as you read this section. If you need some inspiration, the Fedora Linux release schedule[3] has over 250 entries.

Each of the following subsections will include a few schedule entry examples. Table 8, Project release schedule, on page 93 puts them together into a final schedule. The example is based on a six-month release cycle with a calendar-based schedule. This schedule targets a release on October 26, 2021.

Define Milestones in Relation to Others

You'll find your life is a lot easier if you define all of the milestones in relation to others. The dependency chain should eventually bring you back to the release date. If you define the code freeze as "four weeks before release," for example, it'll remain accurate if the planned release day shifts.

---

3.   https://fedorapeople.org/groups/schedule/

Prereleases

Releasing before you release is a great way to get testing and feedback from the most engaged parts of your user community. See Development, on page 74 for more about prerelease milestones.

- *Alpha release.* Alpha releases give users a general "this is where we're going" feel. Now that the bravest users can easily run from your development tree, a lot of projects have abandoned the alpha release. But if you think an alpha release makes sense for your project, it's best to do it early. You'll want to have your features planned and at least partially implemented so alpha users have something to give you feedback on, but you want to leave yourself plenty of time to react to the feedback. Two-fifths of the way through the development cycle is a good starting point. More conservative projects will do alpha releases even sooner—Python starts alpha releases five months into a 17-month development cycle.

- *Beta release.* For most large projects, a beta release is standard. The length of time between the beta release and the final release depends on the scale of your project and the length of the development cycle. Whether by coincidence or natural fit, many projects release a beta about five-sixths of the way between releases. KDE Plasma (4-month release cadence), GNOME (6-month release cadence), and Fedora Linux (6-month release cadence) all follow this pattern. On the other hand, if your project is a major building block where bugs can have long-lived effects, you may choose to go longer. Python, with a 12-month release cadence, starts beta releases five months before the final release.

Milestone	Date
Beta release	2021-09-21
Final release	2021-10-26

Table 1—Pre- and final release milestones

Development

There's a bit of a circular dependency between this part and Create the Timeline, on page 108. You can use either the features process to set the development milestones in the schedule or the schedule to constrain the features process's timeline. In reality, you'll probably adjust your features process and the schedule a few times as you work on your first few releases. For now, it's enough to pencil these milestones in so you can fine-tune them once the features process is complete.

- *Feature planning.* Depending on what your project's features process looks like, you'll probably have some kind of deadline for planning. This may include proposals, approvals, or "hey, this is what I'm going to do!" announcements.

- *Feature completion.* As every student knows, at some point it's time to put the pencil down. Similarly, somewhere on your schedule, it's time to stop coding and start shipping. You may choose, as Fedora does, to have multiple completion deadlines. The first deadline is for the feature to be complete enough that the QA team can start testing all of the functionality. Soon thereafter, the second deadline is for 100% code completion.

Milestone	Date
Feature proposal deadline	2021-07-20
Code completion deadline	2021-08-24

Table 2—Development milestones

Testing

Most mature projects perform automated testing on a regular basis. Often, code has to not only build but also pass integration tests before it can be merged. Even with automated testing, some features still need a human to break them. Which features or use cases in your project are hard to test in an automated way?

- *Code freezes.* It's much easier to test code that's stable (as in unchanging). Prior to a release (including prereleases), you want to freeze the code base to give testers a consistent target to test against. Some projects look at it from the opposite direction. The Linux kernel, for example, has "merge windows" where code is allowed to be merged into the mainline kernel. A merge window is the part of the schedule that isn't under a code freeze.
- *Test days.* Test days are a great way to build community while also getting real-world testing on your project. Depending on the size and complexity, you might test the whole thing or focus on specific areas. Schedule test days far enough into the development cycle that there's something to actually test, but leave yourself time to fix any issues before the release day.

Milestone	Date
Beta freeze begins	2021-08-24
Final freeze	2021-10-05

Table 3—Testing milestones

Marketing

You might think of marketing as an unnecessary activity in an open source project. But if you don't tell people about your project, how will they find out about it? Marketing starts long before the release. Even if you don't start talking publicly about the release, you have to prepare to be ready on the release day.

- *Press briefing.* If your project gets coverage in the tech press (or if you wish it did), you'll want to have a briefing out to your favorite journalists in advance of the release. A detailed description is beyond the scope of this book. For our purposes, let's say that you can't spell "news" without "new." This is a milestone you'd like to hit so that your release gets a big splash on the release day. The target for sending it should be 2–3 business days before the release date, but ideally not until the go/no-go decision has been made. You may want to start the process a week prior to release to collect the relevant facts, quotes, and screenshots you want to pass along.

- *Release announcement.* You want to have a release announcement ready for your project's mailing list, forum, blog, what have you. While it doesn't strictly need to be available until the release day, setting a deadline of 3–4 days gives time for it to come in "late" and still be on time.

- *Websites.* If your project's website highlights the features of the latest release, you'll want to have those updates ready to publish on the release day. A content submission deadline a week or so before the release (or a month if it involves design changes) gives your websites team a chance to edit and test the changes.

- *Swag.* Most of the time, you're probably not refreshing your swag with every release. But for significant releases (10th anniversary, totally redone UI, and so on), you might want to have new stickers, socks, cups, or whatever. If you want this to be available on the release day, you'll need to check your vendor's delivery times. But as general advice, having the designs ready by two months prior to release is a reasonable starting point.

- *Talking points.* When your community members represent your project in conference booths or other situations, it helps to give them prepared talking points. This tells them what to highlight when they talk about your project. Have them ready two weeks before the release because they'll help with writing content for the press briefing and release announcement.

Milestone	Date
Talking points deadline	2021-10-12
Website content updates due	2021-10-19
Release announcement deadline	2021-10-22

Table 4—Marketing milestones

Documentation

Like marketing, documentation is an exercise that should begin in advance of the release day.

- *Release notes.* Release notes are the bare minimum for documentation. With the exception of a "known bugs" section, the features process in Chapter 9, Manage Features, on page 99 should provide most of the content. Plan a release notes content deadline about a week before the release (including alpha and beta releases if you're doing those).

- *Guides validation.* If your project produces guides or other long-form documentation, audit these for accuracy with every release. Starting that process around the beta release (or where the beta release would be if you choose not to do beta releases) should give the team enough time to validate the content.

Watch for Late Changes

From the time the release notes are written up until the release goes out, changes might occur that will affect the release notes. A feature might be pulled at the last minute or it may be modified to avoid unintended behavior. The documentation team will need to be informed of these changes. As the program manager, you're well-situated to make sure that communication is happening—even if you're not doing it yourself.

Milestone	Date
Beta release notes deadline	2021-09-14
Final release notes deadline	2021-10-21

Table 5—Documentation milestones

Translation

There's no universal language, so many projects have translators for the code, documentation, website, and so on.

- *String freeze.* Translators need time to do their work. In the same way you have a code freeze for testers, you need a string freeze for translators. If you have an early code completion deadline as previously described, that's a good time to schedule the string freeze. If not, a week or two before the code freeze is a good starting point. You can freeze strings as late as the start of the code freeze—especially if the changes in strings are minimal—but in general, it's better to give your translators extra time to do the work.

- *Translations due.* The timing for this varies based on what's being translated. Websites can be updated at any time, so you might choose to not have a deadline at all and publish the translations as they're available. (It's friendlier to have translations available on the release day, so you should prefer that whenever possible.) Software that doesn't have QA tests run in translated languages should have translations due when it's time to build the release candidate. If you do QA (either automated or manual) on the translated languages, the translations should be due in time to run the validation tests. Halfway between the start of the string freeze and the beginning of release candidate production is a good starting point.

Milestone	Date
String freeze	2021-09-28
Translations due	2021-10-08

Table 6—Translation milestones

Release Candidates

Even though you've been testing all along, you still want to double-check before you ship the release. For some projects, the release candidates are public deliverables published for wide feedback from the user community. Other projects use release candidates internally—the release candidate is the exact code that will ship if the final validation tests pass. In the former case, you'll want several release candidate milestones on the schedule ahead of the release milestones. The length can vary from a day or two for small projects to several weeks or a month for larger, more conservative projects. In the latter case, the release candidate milestone can fall before the go/no-go decision. Be sure to put it far enough before that so you can run all of your validation tests without keeping the QA team up all night. See Produce Release Candidates, on page 142 to help you figure out your approach to release candidates. The schedule example we're building in this chapter assumes two release candidates planned a few days apart.

Milestone	Date
Release candidate #1	2021-10-19
Release candidate #2	2021-10-21

Table 7—Release candidate milestones

Release Milestones

You can take two approaches with release milestones. The first is to pick a date that you're absolutely certain that you'll hit, even if you encounter some unexpected problems in testing. The second is to pick a date that you think you can hit, with some alternate dates that more closely reflect reality. The single-date approach avoids the embarrassment of missing the release date. On the other hand, it means that you potentially have a lot of idle time where your code waits around.

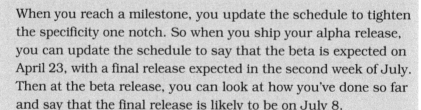

Be Strategically Vague

Feature-based schedules enable you to use vaguely defined dates to your advantage. Because you know that your estimates have uncertainty, you can be fuzzy with the dates as you get further out. For each major milestone, take some precision off of your estimate.

As an example, if you're starting the development process on January 1, you might set the schedule with day specificity through the alpha release on February 28. From there, you know you'll probably do the beta release in the fourth week of April. The final release will come in the third quarter of the year.

When you reach a milestone, you update the schedule to tighten the specificity one notch. So when you ship your alpha release, you can update the schedule to say that the beta is expected on April 23, with a final release expected in the second week of July. Then at the beta release, you can look at how you've done so far and say that the final release is likely to be on July 8.

If you're used to Agile development, this concept will seem familiar. It builds in the understanding that you can't predict with certainty how long development will take. This way your schedule reflects the inherent uncertainty.

Depending on how you handle release life cycles (see *Develop Your Release Life Cycle*), this may mean you accumulate a larger pool of changes postrelease that will grow increasingly destabilizing. If you choose the multiple-dates approach, be clear about the early one being a "preferred" or "early" target. Fedora Linux calls the second date "target date #1" and considers hitting that date as being "on-time."

The Final Schedule

Now that we've identified all of the milestones, let's put them together to form the final schedule. Depending on the size of your community and the number of entries, you may choose to have versions of the schedule that represent a particular subset. Here's the final version of the sample schedule we've worked on in this section.

Milestone	Date
Feature proposal deadline	2021-07-20
Code completion deadline	2021-08-24
Beta freeze begins	2021-08-24
Beta release notes deadline	2021-09-14
Beta release	2021-09-21
String freeze	2021-09-28
Translations due	2021-10-08
Final freeze	2021-10-05
Talking points deadline	2021-10-12
Website content updates due	2021-10-19
Release candidate #1	2021-10-19
Final release notes deadline	2021-10-21
Release candidate #2	2021-10-21
Release announcement deadline	2021-10-22
Final release	2021-10-26

Table 8—Project release schedule

Manage Conflicts

Problem: As soon as you produce a schedule, someone asks for a change or an external event throws it off.

The milestones in your schedule are in constant tension. When one needs to change, you have to manage the trade-offs in the rest of the schedule to accommodate the change. Let's look at how you can do that.

You want your schedule to be as efficient as possible so you get the release into your users' hands as quickly as possible. But you also want it to have some slack so you can accommodate bad estimates and unexpected delays without requiring your community to forego sleep.

After you've built your schedule but before you've started working against it, there's one more task: evaluate it for conflicts. You can't know in advance what unexpected events will pop up at inconvenient times. But you can at least plan for the expected events.

Accommodating External Conflicts

Problem: An external event pops up in the middle of a key part of your schedule.

What sorts of disruptive events can you expect? Well, events for one—as in conferences. If there's a conference that's popular in your community (or among a key subset), you shouldn't expect a lot of work to happen during it. It might be good to make minor adjustments to milestones to accommodate—either before the conference or after.

Holidays are also potential schedule-wreckers. They're complicated, though. When do *you* have the most time to contribute to your project? Is it when you're at work or is it over a holiday break? Is that true for everyone else?

Some of your contributors may have more time to devote to your project on a holiday since they're off work. Others may be busy with family and contribute less than normal. And of course, neither public nor religious holidays are universally observed. I'm told there are even some people who don't observe Star Wars Day!

The last week of December is probably the closest thing we have to a universal holiday, as many cultures and countries have at least one holiday associated with the winter solstice, Gregorian new year, or religious celebrations. Measurements of contributions to Fedora Linux show a sharp drop in that week, although still nonzero, as shown in the contribution graph on page 95. It's best not to try to adjust your schedule too much to accommodate holidays; if you move a date to avoid one holiday, you'll likely land on another. Also, be aware that milestones timed around holidays frequently observed in your community may need a little flexibility.

Making Adjustments

Problem: You have to make a change to the schedule, but you don't know how to adjust other parts of the schedule to accommodate the change.

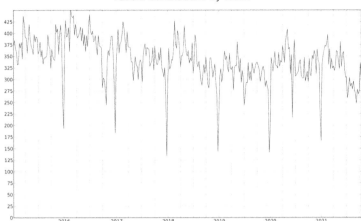

Fedora Contributors by Week

Changing a milestone requires either changing others or compressing a period. For example, if you decide to delay the code freeze due because everyone is too far behind, you need to either delay any milestones that come after (including the release day) or shorten the testing period. Depending on how much you delay the freeze, you may choose one option or the other. The answer to "can we change this date on the schedule?" isn't "yes," it's "yes, if…." What will the impact be on the schedule—and therefore the community—if you make that change?

As a concrete example, the Fedora Linux beta freeze ends on the day of the beta release. The early target date is five weeks before the early final target. The final freeze starts two weeks before the early final target. When the beta release hits the early target, the result is a three-week "thaw" where updates can reach the repo. Hitting the target date #1 for beta shortens the thaw to two weeks. We consider that a good trade-off for keeping the final release on track. If the beta is delayed enough that the beta freeze ends at the same time the final freeze begins, then we may consider giving up on the early final target and starting the final freeze a week late.

Keep the Schedule Accurate

Problem: You missed a milestone, so the schedule is no longer accurate.

Your job isn't over when the schedule is done. When have you ever been a part of something that has gone exactly to plan? As time progresses, reality has a way of diverging from what you expected. It's up to you as the program manager to notice this divergence and act on it.

Why might the schedule become wrong? The most common problem is that it took longer than expected to do the work. Estimates are hard. I had a professor who liked to say "multiply your estimate by three and then you'll only be half as wrong." That's a little cynical, but it highlights a good point: you'll almost always underestimate how long something takes. This is particularly true the first time you do something. With repetition, you will get better at estimating.

This means that after a few releases, your release engineering team will get pretty good at knowing how long it takes to build a release candidate. The QA team can tell you how long it takes to go through the validation tests. Most of the project will be relatively predictable unless it has an abnormally large set of changes between releases. But the feature development will remain largely unpredictable. That's not because software engineers are particularly bad at estimating, but because the nature of the work necessarily involves novelty. As you get several releases under your belt, you'll find that the development estimates don't become as predictable as the rest.

To bring the schedule in line with the new reality, you need to consult the contingency plans for each feature. This will be discussed more later when you create the features process on page 100. For now, it's sufficient to know that you have a few general choices.

For calendar-based schedules, you can adjust the incomplete features by deferring them to the next release or narrowing the scope (and deferring the rest). If you can safely do so, you can ship with the feature incomplete (for example if the library is mostly written but nothing links to it yet). Or you can choose to delay the release to give the developers more time to complete the feature. This is generally the least appealing option—shipping on time is important to your project's credibility—but for important features (or features that are hard to back out), you may decide this is the best option.

For feature-based schedules, the release date isn't fixed, so you may choose to keep working on it. At some point, though, you do want to get the release out. "Vaporware" isn't a label that most projects want. If nine features out of ten are done and the tenth is still far from complete, you'll be tempted to add a couple of features that were planned for the next release. But what happens when feature 10 is done but features 11 and 12 are halfway done? Do you now wait for them to be done, too? If you have straggler features, it's best to reduce their scope or defer them to the next release once it becomes clear that they're not going to be done soon.

Communicate the Schedule

Problem: The community doesn't know when the schedule milestones are. This leads to missed deadlines or unnecessary last-minute effort.

People need to know about the schedule if you want them to meet the deadlines. That means you have to communicate it.

But communicating the schedule is the scariest part. You already know it's going to be wrong, especially the first few times. You just read that releasing on schedule is important for your project's credibility, and you don't want to risk that. People can't say you released late if they don't know when you were planning on releasing. Brilliant! Of course, what use is a schedule that no one knows about?

Publish the schedule somewhere easily accessible in a way that's easy for people to understand it. You want people to be able to refer to it on their own instead of having to ask you every time. If you're developing each schedule independently, announce it prominently wherever it is that your project makes internal announcements as soon as it's ready. If you use a repetitive schedule, announce the new schedule when it starts. For example, I announced the Fedora Linux 35 schedule when Fedora Linux 34 branched from the development ("Rawhide") tree. This marked the real beginning of Fedora Linux 35 development, even though it was a little over two months before the release of 34. In either case, repeat announcements when major milestones are coming up and any time the schedule changes. If you publish a regular status update as described in the Provide Updates, on page 31, include the upcoming milestones as a regular feature. It's almost impossible to overcommunicate upcoming milestones.

For projects with a division of labor among different teams, the schedule naturally gets pretty lengthy. It helps if you provide each team with a view of the schedule with their tasks and milestones. Similarly, highlight the key milestones, either with conspicuous formatting or as a separate schedule view. If you keep your schedule easily consumable, you'll help contributors meet the deadlines as you approach release day.

Retrospective

The release schedule doesn't have to be an unbreakable commitment—it's more of a plan that you make together. Like the release itself, it's a collaborative process. You need input from the teams in your project. Your job as the program manager isn't to dictate the schedule. Instead, you're the scheduling expert who helps the rest of the community understand where their work fits in. You have to take the broad view of the project and help strike the right balance when there are competing interests.

Now that you have your release schedule planned out, it's time to figure out what will go into the release. The next chapter builds on some of the deadlines you defined in the schedule to put together a feature-planning process.

## CHAPTER 9

Manage Features

Once you know what the release schedule looks like, you're ready to define the process for planning features. Your project's feature-planning process is an important tool for planning and coordination. Documenting the planned work allows for early feedback and lets you see when two developers are working on features that overlap or conflict. It also gives the project's documentation and marketing teams an early start on their work.

Of course, you can get by without a features process. Many open source projects do. Those projects let developers do what they're doing and merge the features when they're ready. But how do you know what's coming? What do you do if two people are working on mutually exclusive features?

Skipping a features process is fine if the project is just you or you and a few friends. The larger the project gets, the more likely it is that you'll need to coordinate how some of the features land. At the very least, other developers will want to know a change is coming so they can adjust their work appropriately. Remember how we discussed the increase in communication overhead as a project grows? You combat that, in part, by having a centralized feature-planning process.

Don't confuse "centralize" with "top-down," though. The process shouldn't impose a plan on contributors. Your project remains a "do-ocracy"; the people doing the work decide what they're doing. It's the information and communication that you're centralizing, not the planning.

Additionally, one of the benefits of open source is the fact that many people have eyes on the code. Wouldn't you agree that community-wide discussion of planned features is a natural extension of this? When you give the community input on plans, they not only feel more engaged, but they also find weaknesses you overlooked. You can see how the benefits of a well-designed process outweigh the costs.

This chapter draws heavily from two well-tested and documented processes: Fedora's Changes process[1] and Python's PEP-1.[2] While you could certainly build your process from a blank page using this chapter, you might prefer to start with one of those two and use the concepts in this chapter to help you make the changes appropriate for your project. After all, if you can reuse code, you can reuse processes as well.

Create a Template

Problem: Contributors submit their feature plans with no consistency or structure. Critical information gets left out of the initial proposal.

Before developing a process for how to handle feature proposals, let's figure out what a feature proposal is. For a lightweight process, a proposal might be a simple email that says "I'm going to do *blah.*" But to get the most value from the process, be specific about what it is you want the proposer to communicate. Since you're enumerating this information anyway, you might as well make a template. This simplifies everyone's life. The template on page 102 shows a contrived example of what a feature proposal template might look like.

Encourage Preproposals

 You don't need to require a fully formed proposal to begin discussing a feature idea. In fact, it's better to encourage people to informally discuss their ideas before writing the proposal. This helps the feature owner refine their ideas and get a sense of what the community sentiment will be. An idea that's already been through a few discussions and iterations will generally go through the formal feature proposal process more smoothly.

The following information should be part of every feature process.

• *Name.* It seems obvious, but naming the proposal helps you communicate about the proposal. Think of it as the subject of an email. One important point is that the name should be unique over time. "Update the GUI library to version 6" is a much better name than "update the GUI library."

---

1.   https://docs.fedoraproject.org/en-US/program_management/changes_policy/

2.   https://www.python.org/dev/peps/pep-0001/

- *Summary.* This is a short (from a sentence or two up to a paragraph) description of the proposal. This should focus on the "what" of the proposal, not the "why."

- *Owner.* Who is responsible for this feature and how should others contact them? The owner can be a team (for example, the user interface group), but at least one individual should be listed to act as the representative.

- *Benefit to the project.* Why is this feature important? Does it make life better for the developers? For the users?

- *Scope.* The section Create the Timeline, on page 108 talks about the possibility of having different submission deadlines based on a category of scope. If you create that for your project, proposals should state the category in this section. In either case, the scope section should include what areas of the code or the project are affected. This may be particular subsystems of the code or other development teams that will need to do work in response to this feature.

- *Dependencies.* What does this proposal require from other individuals or teams in order to be implemented? Those people should be notified and on board with the proposal before it goes through the process.

- *Test plan.* The QA team will want to know this. In addition, you may publish this with an alpha or beta release so that users can know what to test for the feature.

- *Contingency plan.* If the feature is incomplete at the deadline, how will it be handled? For that matter, what is the appropriate deadline? Features with a broad scope may need a contingency date at the alpha freeze, whereas a small feature that stands in isolation might be able to wait until the beta release.

In addition to these items, consider asking for proposals to also include the following information. You may choose to make some optional, depending on the needs of your project, or conditional on the scope of the proposal.

- *Category.* You may have slightly different paths or requirements depending on the type of feature. For example, Fedora distinguishes between "System-Wide Changes," which impact the entire distribution, and "Self-Contained Changes," which are handled by a single contributor or team. System-Wide Changes require a few fields that are optional for Self-Contained Changes and face a higher standard of scrutiny when it comes time to evaluate contingency plans. Python's PEP-1 defines three types of proposals:[3] "Standards Track," "Informational," and "Process." These distinguish whether a proposal covers, for example, a new feature of the language or a new way of building Python.

- *Compatibility and upgrades.* This section should describe any backward-incompatible changes to be made. In addition, it describes changes to existing behavior or interventions required of the user after an upgrade.

- *Rationale.* This builds on the "benefit to the project" section from the previous list, which explained why the feature owner is making the proposal. Proposals should describe the decisions that led to the scope and benefits listed. In particular, they should describe why alternative options were rejected. The community will invariably ask "why didn't you..." on the mailing list, so it saves everyone time to preempt that conversation.

- *Release notes.* Give the writers of the release notes a nudge in the direction they should go. This doesn't have to be the final content of the release notes. It's there simply as a guide.

- *Documentation.* If the feature brings in external code, link to the upstream documentation. Include any design documents, blog posts, and so on where the concepts have been explained. Give the documentation writers ideas on what should be covered in the project's docs.

- *Downsides.* Talk about what the negatives are for this new feature. Does it weaken the security profile for the user? Does it enable abuse or harassment?

- *Feedback.* If the proposal was discussed prior to being written, what was the reaction?

Here's an example of a feature proposal template (in Markdown) with sample data:

```
# Feature proposal: Add a sudoku

## Summary
Add the ability for users to solve a sudoku while a database query runs.

## Owner
Pro Grammer (pro.grammer@example.com)

## Benefit to the project
Database queries are slow as molasses. If we distract the users with a
puzzle to solve, maybe they won't notice.
```

---

3.   https://www.python.org/dev/peps/pep-0001/#pep-types

```
## Scope
Minor feature
This only affects the web interface.

## Dependencies
The UI team needs to add support for rendering the puzzle. I'll add
the library for generating puzzles.

## Test plan
1. Load webpage
2. Solve sudoku
3. Hit refresh

## Contingency plan
If this isn't ready for the Beta freeze, I'll revert any changes.

## Compatibility and upgrades
This proposal does not introduce any incompatibilities.

## Rationale
Fixing the query performance seems hard. Adding a sudoku is easy.

## Release notes
Version 1.2.3 generates a sudoku to solve while the database query
runs.

## Documentation
None (unless we want to link to the Wikipedia article)

## Downsides
Generating a sudoku in the browser may slow the user's machine.

## Feedback
I brought this up at a local meetup group and they all loved it.
```

Now that you've made your feature proposal template, it's time to develop the process to handle the proposals.

Set the Scale

Problem: The process is too heavy for the trivial features and too light for the complicated features.

No one process works for every project. The smaller your project is—specifically the number of contributors—the less process you'll probably need. Your job as the program manager is to get the process at the right level for your community's needs. Let's look at how to do that.

Harvard professor Richard Hackman observed[4] that the number of communication channels in a team goes up exponentially with the number of people

---

4.   https://hbr.org/2009/05/why-teams-dont-work

on the team. In community-driven projects, this becomes even more complicated as people come and go, and even your long-time contributors might not be checking in every day. The feature process is here to consolidate those communication channels into a single area where people can quickly check to see if they care and then get back to whatever it is they do.

At one end of the scale are the solo developer hobby projects. The feature process there is "I pick something I want to work on, probably make a git branch for it if I remember, merge it, and tag a release when I'm out of stuff that I can/want to do." At the other end is an operating system like Fedora Linux. Despite its name, the "Fedora Project" isn't a single project; it's a program of related projects that mostly move in the same direction. Hundreds of people per week may touch a Linux distribution in a technical sense: updating package specs, creating builds, performing manual tests, and so on. This doesn't even include the untold people who work in the upstream projects.

These upstreams all have their own release schedules and their own processes for how features land and when. Nobody can keep up with everything on their own, so the features process brings important changes to light. The important thing to remember is that the process is there to serve the community. The community isn't there to serve the process. As you read the rest of the section, ask yourself if each part makes sense for your project. It's okay if the answer is "no."

Set the Approval Process

Problem: There's no clear way to determine if a feature proposal will be included or not.

Does the very notion of an "approval process" evoke a sense of horror? It might. But it shouldn't if you do it right.

For many projects, developers willing to do the work simply get to do the work. People often find the inherent autonomy in open source projects as important as anything else. And for smaller projects, an explicit process for approval is probably too heavy. What's important is for that to be an intentional decision. As your project grows, you may need to shift to a more formal process.

As you read in Chapter 5, Design Suitable Processes, on page 43, you need to consider who gets a *voice* and who gets a *vote*. These aren't inherently the same group, although they can be. In general, you want your project to have a broad group of people with a voice so that the community can provide input.

But when it comes time to take a vote, a smaller group will be able to arrive at a decision much more quickly.

Define Who Has a Voice

Problem: You want to make sure the relevant people have the opportunity to comment on a feature proposal.

One of the first things to consider when putting together a feature management process for your community is: "who needs to review feature proposals?" As you saw earlier, this doesn't necessarily mean approving the changes. Are there people who should take a look early in the process? Maybe your release engineering or infrastructure teams need to review them to make sure they don't require changes to the build infrastructure. Maybe you have a legal review process to make sure licenses are in order. Perhaps you act as the proposal wrangler to make sure all of the required information is included.

These pre-reviews are helpful to ensure that the proposal isn't an immediate no-go. If the feature involves adding code incompatible with your project's license, no amount of community discussion is going to make it workable. A feature that breaks the way you build the project isn't necessarily a show-stopper—after all, maybe that's the point of the change—but you want to make sure that's intentional, or at least understood by the submitter. The point of these early checks is to not waste the full community's time discussing a proposal that's not ready.

The next step is to decide who in the community provides feedback. You can choose to present proposals to the full community or have a select group provide feedback. In most cases, it's best to let the full community weigh in. Open source projects have contributors with a variety of expertise working in parts of the project you might not expect. You never know where good ideas might come from, so why not let everyone weigh in?

Because you are giving everyone a voice, you are increasing the sense of engagement your contributors have. People like knowing that their voices can be heard. You're asking for advisory input, not approval, so you don't need to get everyone's buy-in. Full consensus isn't necessary (or possible in most cases), but if there's a large outcry, that may tell you something.

One example of this in action is a Fedora Linux proposal submitted a few years ago. Fedora, like many open source projects, has no reliable way of knowing how many computers run the software. The project leader submitted a proposal that would generate a unique ID for each installed system and optionally report that when checking the repository for updates. By counting the number of unique IDs that appear, it's possible to know how many Fedora Linux machines exist in the world. Or at least how many are checking for updates.

When this proposal hit the community mailing list, a lot of people expressed concern. Although the unique ID didn't contain any information about the system or the user, it still was tied to a specific machine. Some community members expressed concern about it being a General Data Privacy Regulation (GDPR) issue. Others worried that if the ID database were to leak, the IDs could be tied to the IP address and thus to the user.

In light of these concerns, the proposal's owner reworked his plan. The new version had the update tool send a "count me" message along with the repository metadata request once a week. This traded off a little bit of accuracy in the count for a better privacy message. By catching this issue before any code had been written, the community improved the feature.

Define Who Has a Vote

Problem: You don't have a clear definition of who can approve feature proposals.

Even if your project lacks any sort of organizational structure, someone ends up approving features. The simplest form of approval is when the person who proposed the feature implements it. Easy-peasy! In loosely organized communities, that might work. Fully democratic communities might put it to a community-wide vote. If a certain number or proportion of members vote in favor, the feature is approved. Other communities may give that power to an individual or group. They could be responsible for the entire project or certain subsections. This is common in the "benevolent dictator for life" governance model used by some projects.

Whatever approval method you choose should reflect the norms and values of your community. For any project with a significant contributor base, a model where a small body makes approval decisions is usually the right approach. A pure democracy can be pretty messy. When was the last time you got the entire community to agree to something? And pure democracy is subject to "brigading," where someone brings along a large group of otherwise uninterested people to support their position. People who may have no familiarity with the technical ramifications of a proposal will be able to cast a binding vote.

In the Fedora Project, feature proposal approval is the role of the Fedora Engineering Steering Committee (FESCo). This is a 9-person body entirely elected by community members. By electing members, the community has the ability to remove members who aren't acting in the best interests of the project. But having a small group enables relatively quick decisions without a large overhead.

Define How Features Are Enforced

Problem: Multiple contributors propose mutually exclusive features. Incomplete features linger, delaying the release.

What happens if two proposed features are in conflict? Or if implementing a feature turns out to have a negative impact? Someone needs to have the authority to say "this isn't going in after all" or to make sure conflicting changes are brought into agreement. This is another advantage of having a defined approval body.

Your quality assurance team and processes will be a part of this, and maybe they're the ones who make the final call. If the feature isn't complete by the deadline, it doesn't go in. It's relatively straightforward to come up with a plan for what to do if a feature doesn't work as expected or is incomplete by the deadline. If you required a contingency plan as part of the feature process, then implement that plan.

The harder part is what happens if someone makes a change that doesn't go through your feature process? Here's a secret of open source program management: you can't force people to go through your process. So if something sneaks in and you don't discover it until you have a release candidate, you have a few options: you can let it in or you can get someone to forcibly remove it. In either case, you'll have someone who is unhappy. It's either the person who made the change because you kicked their work out or the people who had to deal with the breakage it caused. (If it snuck in without anyone noticing, then it's probably not that big of a deal.)

The solution to avoiding or violating the features process is social pressure. All of an open source project's rules ultimately rely on contributors following the project's norms. Processes are sometimes painful to follow, but a well-designed and well-maintained process will give more benefit than it costs. In this case, the benefit may be identifying breakages sooner or giving other developers a chance to take advantage of new features that are offered. And it can help prevent slips in the release schedule or an unnecessary heroic effort from your QA team.

As the program manager, enforcing the process is your responsibility. When you talk about the process—particularly when addressing a violation—emphasize the benefits of following the process. This includes the benefits to the developers using the process and the community as a whole. If you can't articulate a benefit of a particular part of the process, that's a good sign that you should consider modifying or eliminating it. In addition, watch for the things people regularly skip or skimp on. This is a warning that the value in that step is not evident.

Create the Timeline

Problem: The community doesn't know when to expect features to land—or not.

As you saw when adding development milestones to your schedule on page 87, your features process is critical to the whole release. The elements of the features process feed the rest of the schedule. This is why it's important for you to define the process timeline.

Open the Proposal Window

Problem: Feature owners aren't sure when they can submit proposals.

The first milestone on the timeline is opening the window for feature proposals. This lets developers know they can begin submitting their feature proposals. In many projects, this isn't an explicit milestone. Developers may submit proposals as far in advance as they'd like so long as it's clear what version they're targeting. This requires, or at least strongly suggests, that your project works on multiple releases in parallel. If that's not the case, or if you want to avoid confusion, you may choose to explicitly begin to allow feature proposals. The proposal window should open as early as possible in the release cycle.

Close the Proposal Window

Problem: No one knows when it's too late for submitting a feature proposal. Proposals may come in at the very last minute, delaying the release or causing additional heroic work.

The next milestone on the timeline is closing the window for feature proposals. To be clear, this is the deadline for *submitting* the proposal, not for completing the work. This deadline should happen well in advance of the code completion deadline you set on your schedule.

You might choose to have multiple proposal deadlines depending on the scope of the work and the impact on other parts of the project. As a result, features that require other developers to do work (for example, moving to the next major release of a library) or that present a significant change to the infrastructure should have an earlier deadline. Features where one developer (or team of developers) does the work in isolation can fall later in the schedule. You may find yourself tempted to come up with many deadlines based on a complicated array of factors. Don't. The idea is to give developers as much time as possible to submit their proposals without making the process overly complicated.

When planning your deadlines, consider the length of the approval process. Make sure there's time between when the proposal is approved and when the feature needs to land. If your approval process takes four weeks, don't make the deadline for proposals that require a massive rebuild two weeks before the rebuild begins. Approval processes don't always take the advertised amount of time, so a buffer of 1.5 to 2 times the nominal time is a good starting point.

Check for Completion

Problem: Feature owners don't know when they have to complete their work. Major changes land during supposed freezes, complicating QA work.

As you read previous sections of this chapter, you realized that an approved proposal is not the end of the features process. Now it's time to make sure they stay on track. At the code completion deadlines, you set in the previous chapter on page 87, you need to see which features are still incomplete. For each of these incomplete features, look at the contingency plan and see what needs to be done. In some cases, leaving the feature incomplete does no harm. In other cases, the developer may need to roll back their changes or put a mitigation in place.

Whatever method you use to approve changes should also be used to determine the course of action for incomplete changes. In some cases, it may be better to grant the feature a deadline extension. In others, you might need to reduce the scope or defer the change to the next release. No matter what the final decision is, as a program manager you need to make sure the decision is communicated across the project. In particular, you want to let the marketing and documentation teams know not to write up the feature. You may also want to let the QA team know that they won't need to test the feature—or that they should test to make sure it was removed successfully.

If you have prereleases (alphas and betas) before your final release, you might break up your milestones across those phases of development. For an alpha release, you may choose not to require any specific degree of completeness. Often, you want it to be at least roughly complete so that your earliest testers can provide meaningful feedback, but if there are a dozen features, it may not matter if any specific one is less complete than planned. Once you reach the beta release, the features should be complete enough for testing. Ideally, they'll be fully code complete, but you may exempt certain pieces. By the time you're ready for the final release, of course, you'll want all of the code complete. In general, the time between beta and final releases should be focused on fixing bugs and polishing the rough edges, not implementing the feature.

Define the Life Cycle of a Proposal

Problem: The timeline for proposals is unclear. Inconsistent handling leads to feelings of unfair treatment or exclusion of less-frequent contributors.

Do you like "hurry up and wait?" I didn't think so, and your community doesn't either. Proposals should not languish for the entire length of the release's proposal window. Move proposals through the process expeditiously so that the feature owners can get to work on implementation.

Each proposal has its own mini-milestones attached. The first is the beginning of the community comment (the "voice") period, which is generally when you announce the proposal on the mailing list or other appropriate venue. This is the best time for the general community (including both developers and users) to provide comments and critiques because the implementation work hasn't started.

Be clear about how long the community comment period lasts. You can choose to wait until the discussion has stopped, but some threads carry on well past the point of any constructive dialogue. And then people get upset because they feel like you cut them off. If you set a time limit, it's unambiguous. One or two weeks is probably sufficient in most cases. Any shorter and you exclude people who are spending a few days offline or who are limited in the time they can devote to the project. Any longer and you either have "dead air" (no one is commenting because the proposal is uncontroversial or all of the disagreements are settled) or the conversation is probably going in circles.

At the end of the community comment period, it's time for the voting period. This could start immediately after the comment period ends, or you may include a brief delay so that the proposal's owner can make adjustments based on the feedback. Even if you have a small group that does the actual voting (so that you know exactly how many votes there are to count), it's best to put a time limit on this. You don't want to hold up an obvious outcome because one person decided to take a week away from the keyboard. See Take a Vote, on page 39 for more on voting processes.

If the approval body approves the proposal, then the feature owner gets to work implementing the plan. If not, the owner may rework the proposal to address the rejection reasons and resubmit.

Shepherd the Proposals

Problem: Feature owners deal with the process infrequently, so they skip steps or leave off information.

How well do you remember the steps of a process you rarely do? Not well, right? That's true for most people. Getting through a process smoothly requires familiarity and experience. So name one or several "feature wranglers."

These aren't gatekeepers so much as shepherds. You don't necessarily give them the ability to approve or reject proposals, but they are responsible for moving the proposals through the process. As the program manager, this will probably fall to you by default. But you can delegate this duty.

The shepherd's job is to check the proposal for completeness and correctness. You don't need to pass technical judgment on the content of the proposal, but you do need to ensure that it contains all of the required information. Because you're trying to make the process as low-friction as possible, you might choose to start a proposal through the process with information missing. For example, if your process requires suggested release notes content, you might announce a proposal to the community but tell the owner that you won't submit it to the approval body until that section is complete.

The shepherd should also be responsible for announcing the proposal in the appropriate venue for community review (for example, the development mailing list). When it's ready for submission to the approval body, the shepherd handles the submission. If the proposal is approved, the shepherd should open a tracking issue, including issues for the project's release notes. You can have people wrangle their own changes, but this is a specialized task and benefits from a dedicated person who does this regularly, instead of making community members do it less frequently. The image on page 112 shows a listing from the "Friday's Fedora Facts" posts I do every week on the Fedora Community Blog.[5] Each week, I list the pending feature proposals (Fedora calls them "Changes") and the ones that were approved or rejected in the past week.

Up until the last paragraph, I've carefully managed to avoid talking about the tooling for managing feature proposals. You'll want a tool of some sort: a wiki page, a text file in a git repository, a kanban board, a bug/issue tracker, or

---

5.　https://communityblog.fedoraproject.org

Proposal	Type	Status
Make btrfs the default file system for Fedora Cloud	System-Wide	Approved
Sphinx 4	Self-Contained	Approved
Build Fedora Cloud Images with Hybrid BIOS+UEFI Boot Support	System-Wide	Approved
Replace the Anaconda product configuration files with profiles	Self-Contained	FESCo #2622
Use yescrypt as default hashing method for shadow passwords	System-Wide	FESCo #2623
Python Packaging Guidelines overhaul	System-Wide	Announced
Remove authselect-compat package	System-Wide	Announced

Changes approved, rejected, or withdrawn will be removed from this table the next week. See the ChangeSet page for a full list of approved changes.

a combination of these. The goal is to track the state of the features and provide some easy reporting on their status as they move through the process. This makes it easier to know what is complete, what is at risk, and what needs to be deferred to a later release. You can use whatever works best for your project, but in general, you'll want to minimize copying and pasting and maximize scriptability.

The following figure shows how Fedora tracks features in Bugzilla, with different bug states representing varying levels of completion.

Bug ID Status Resolution Summary [Expand All] [Collapse All] [Load All] [View as Bug l

- 1894270 NEW   Fedora 35 Change proposal tracker
    1598524 ASSIGNED   glibc32 Build Adjustments
    1740811 ASSIGNED   Ship BerkleyDB backend as a module
    1825937 ASSIGNED   OpenSSL3.0
  + 1834844 ASSIGNED   Introduce module Obsoletes and EOL
    1866896 ASSIGNED   Patches in Forge macros - Auto macros
    1889901 ASSIGNED   DNS Over TLS
  + 1890881 MODIFIED   Python 3.10 tracker
    1899998 ASSIGNED   Modular GNOME Keyring services
    1905142 ASSIGNED   Remove nscd
    1906540 MODIFIED   Rename libusb packages and deprecate old API
  + 1915976 ASSIGNED   DNF/RPM Copy on Write enablement for all variants
    1916921 MODIFIED   LTO Build Improvements
    1920226 ASSIGNED   Changes/Binutils 2.36
    1920537 ON_QA   PHP 8.0
    1924101 ASSIGNED   SOF as default audio driver for Intel LPE hardware
    1924737 ASSIGNED   Retire python3.5

Retrospective

Creating a feature-planning process gives your community a way to understand what's coming. It's important as a communication tool as much as anything else. But because it'll feel like unnecessary bureaucracy at times, you need to keep it as lightweight as possible. Adjust the process over time as you learn what works and doesn't work for your community.

With your feature-planning process defined, it's time for the developers to get to work. And writing code generally means bugs. The next chapter looks at how to track and triage your bugs, both during the development cycle and after the release.

## CHAPTER 10

Track and Triage Bugs

You don't *want* bugs in your project, but all nontrivial software has bugs. And enhancement requests. And instances of not-a-bug-but-it-seems-that-way-to-the-users. So while you might intuitively think that a low bug count is good for your project, that's not necessarily the case. In *Producing Open Source Software [Fog17]*, Karl Fogel says a higher number of bug reports reflects better on the project because it shows that people use it.

That's true with a caveat: your bugs can't be stale. If you have a lot of bugs because you have a lot of users, but the bugs get fixed—or at least looked at—that's good. It shows your project has an engaged user community and responsive developers. If the bugs sit forever with no response, you send the message that you don't care. Perhaps the project is abandoned. This chapter will show you how to manage your bugs and know what they say about your project.

Track Bugs

Problem: The bug tracker is a disordered mess. You can't tell any information about the bug reports without reading each of them individually.

From a program management level, you don't care about individual bugs. Your concern is bugs in the aggregate, which means you need to be able to get information about the bugs as a set. This is only possible when you have consistent processes for managing bugs. Let's dig into how to make that happen.

The problem statement at the beginning of this section assumes you already have a bug tracker of some kind. If you don't, fix that first. You'll see more about choosing a bug tracker in Bug Tracker, on page 156, but for now, it's enough to think about the tracker in general terms. Think about what you want to know about your bugs and that will give you a list of requirements when it comes time to pick the tool. Ideally, all of your project's bugs should be in the same tracker so that you can easily aggregate data.

For now, we're only concerned with bugs and enhancement requests—you know, software stuff. Many projects also use bug trackers more broadly to vote on policy or procedures, track meta work, and so on. This is fine, but it's outside the scope of this chapter.

What Is a Bug?

Problem: The community doesn't agree on what constitutes a "bug." Or maybe you're not sure which entries in the bug tracker you should treat as bugs.

"What a silly question, Ben," I hear you say, "I know what a bug is." Of course you do, but in the interest of making sure we're on the same metaphorical page, let's spend a moment coming to a common working definition. A bug is the difference between the *expected* and *actual* behavior of software. When the rm command deletes a file, that's not a bug—it's the purpose of the program. When the ls command deletes a file, that's a big ol' bug.

You may notice that our definition doesn't say *whose* expectations when we defined "bug." That's intentional. A software's users sometimes have different expectations from its developers. This is to be expected and treated with empathy. Your users aren't trying to cause problems; they're trying to use your software. So it's important to consider the "it's not a bug" bugs along with the bugs that everyone agrees are bugs.

"Not a Bug" Reports Are Bugs in Your Docs

 When a bug is closed as "not a bug," it's a waste of the developer's time and a frustration to the user. Instead of getting upset at these sorts of reports, consider that they *are* valid bugs. They're not software bugs—they're documentation bugs. The "not a bug" bug reports are a great place for your documentation team to look when planning documentation improvements.

More challenging are the weird bugs. And you'll get some of those if you're lucky. The most well-known example is XKCD #1172,[1] in which a fictional user's workflow depends on the fact that holding the spacebar down causes the CPU to overheat. That's a contrived example, but I knew a professor who had scripts that (inadvertently) depended on the fact that his shell did not treat numbers that looked like they were in hexadecimal as hexadecimal

---

1.   https://xkcd.com/1172/

numbers. When that bug got fixed, it broke all of his scripts. That was a bug to the user, but a bug fix to the developer. Generally, you'll want to go ahead and consider these sorts of cases in your bug tracking, if for no other reason than it'll be difficult to filter them out.

Strictly speaking, things you want the software to do in the future aren't bugs. But your users might not know they shouldn't expect the software to do that—perhaps other projects already have the functionality. They'll file reports in your bug tracker. Since it's helpful for development and planning to have issues tracked *somewhere*, you'll probably end up using your bug tracker for this, too. For the purposes of this chapter, we'll include feature requests along with bugs.

Bug Attributes

Problem: You are tracking bugs—the actual details of your software's defects—but you don't know what to track *about* the bugs.

A bug report is more than a description of the bug. In fact, the report itself is largely useless to you from a program management perspective. You're interested in the metadata around the bug report. So in this section, let's skip over the "here's what happened versus what I expected to happen" part and talk about the rest of the information you'll want to track.

Similarly, let's take the title as a given. This is a free-form field that's intended to be helpful to humans. It's very difficult to aggregate information from the title or description. You could derail your whole project trying to come up with a natural language parser for bug reports and it still wouldn't get you the right information half the time. Let's agree to resist the urge to require people to encode information into the title. People may commonly use "RFE:" to indicate that it's a request for enhancement instead of a bug, but don't rely on that.

So what attributes should you track?

- *Type.* This is how you track whether something is a bug-bug or a request for enhancement. In addition to "bug" and "enhancement," you might include additional values. For example, "documentation" for docs bugs (assuming you don't treat them separately) or "question" if your bug tracker also serves as a user support platform.

- *Version.* You'll want to know what version of the software the bug report is against. If you decided to limit the versions you support (see Decide How Many, on page 71), a report against an unsupported version can be closed quickly. Similarly, if the report is still open when the release reaches end of life, you can easily find and close it. When analyzing statistics about your bug reports, grouping by version makes it easier to see how you're trending over time. Of course, this information is important to developers when attempting to diagnose and fix the issue, too.

• *Component.* If your project is complex enough to have multiple components, you'll want to know which one the report is against. A component could be a package, an application, or a plugin, depending on the specific context of your project. Whatever "component" means to your project specifically, you can expect that this value will change over the life of a bug report. Sometimes it's because the person filing the report isn't sure of the right component. Other times, a bug appears to be in one component but as the developers look into it they discover the problem lies elsewhere. Smaller or tightly coupled projects probably won't need this field.

• *Platform.* This could be either the CPU architecture, the operating system, or a combination of the two. For GUI applications, it may also include the desktop environment. Often, this information will be more helpful in finding bugs in the upstream libraries you're using. But if your project is working close to the hardware or using operating system calls directly (instead of using, for example, Python's 'os' library), this is more directly relevant to your code. In the absence of user telemetry, the breakdown of bug reports by platform can give you a rough approximation of usage patterns.

• *Status.* The words "open" and "closed" have already made several appearances in this chapter. At a minimum, you should have these two states for bug reports. This allows you to know what bug reports are still valid. Ideally, you should have a few more status options to represent different states. For example, "in progress" for one where an actual person is looking at it and "testing" for when a candidate fix is ready. You might go even more granular and have a status for things like "there's a patch pending review." In general, the administrative overhead outweighs the value of additional statuses beyond the four I suggest.

• *Closure type.* Not all bug report closures are created equal. You'll probably want to distinguish between bugs that were fixed, bugs that couldn't be fixed, bugs that won't be fixed, bugs that aren't actually bugs, and so on. To do this, you'll need to track the closure type. This can be a separate status (for example, "Closed: fixed" versus "Closed: worksforme") or a distinct field that applies to closed bug reports.

- *Impact.* How damaging is this bug? This is a very subjective field because what is a minor inconvenience for one user may break another user's whole workflow. Categories like "low," "medium," and "high" are the best way to capture this information (or at least the least bad way). This field should be the *reporter's* perception of the impact. You can guide them with documentation, but be wary of changing this value on your own, as it's generally a user-hostile behavior.

- *Priority.* This is the *developer's* assessment of where the bug reports rank in the stack of other bug reports to work on. In most cases, categories like the ones previously described for the impact field are sufficient. If you are using a backlog-based workflow, you might end up giving it a unique ranking relative to the other bugs. Ideally, the priority roughly matches the impact. However, there are other factors that affect how quickly a bug gets worked on (see Triage Bugs, on page 120).

- *Time.* At a minimum, you want to know when a bug was opened and when it was closed. This allows you to calculate how long a bug was open. Most bug trackers will give you this without having to make any configuration changes. Knowing how long it takes before someone starts looking at the bug report is helpful, too, but that turns out to be pretty difficult to track in practice. Unless you provide a response time service level agreement (SLA), it's probably not worth the trouble to figure this out (and reports that trigger an SLA should probably be in a dedicated customer support tracker).

- *Reporter.* Who reported the bug? This is another obvious field that almost certainly comes for free in your bug tracker. On its own, it doesn't mean much from a program management perspective. Where it gets interesting is if you have a way of tracking the reporter's affiliation. This is particularly important if your project has a corporation sponsoring (or running) it. If all of the bug reports are coming from the corporation, that suggests you're not attracting the outside community.

- *Assignee.* This field can be tricky, especially if there's a default assignee. The person who fixes the bug isn't necessarily the person a bug report is assigned to. Often, several people play a key part in fixing a bug. That's one of the benefits of open source development. The assignee should be whoever is taking the lead on it at any given moment, and the field should be changed as reality changes. Leaving a bug unassigned is a signal to users that no one is looking into it (and to other contributors that this report may be a good thing for them to pick up).

Give Each Attribute a Field

To make your life easier, give each of the above attributes its own field in the bug tracker. This allows for validation (for example, that the version is an actual version you've released) and consistency. When it comes time to query the report data and do an analysis on it, you'll be glad each field is distinct instead of trying to parse it from a free-form field. Even a simple thing like "put 'RFE' at the beginning of the title" gets complicated when people mix capitalization and sometimes use a colon or surround it in brackets, or spell it out, or...

Triage Bugs

Problem: Nobody is sure which bugs are the important ones. And the problem gets complicated by the presence of duplicate and invalid reports.

You have to do something with a bug once it is opened. To do something with it, you have to make some decisions. How important is it? How easy is the fix? Who has the time and skills to work on it?

In medicine, *triage* is the practice of grouping patients based on the extent of their injuries and their likely mortality. People with minor injuries can wait. People who are almost certain to die aren't treated so that time and resources are focused on those who are critically wounded but could survive. Similarly (except far less emotionally and ethically fraught), bugs that are of trivial impact (for example, a tyop (sic) in a book that doesn't affect the meaning) can wait. A bug that is impossible to fix without shutting everything else down for six months while you rewrite the entire project in a new language won't get much effort. So bug triage involves assessing the impact field described in the previous section in order to set the priority. But there's more to it than that.

Start the process by assessing some basic information: is this actually a bug? Is it a duplicate of an existing report? From there, you can start collecting the information that will allow you to make decisions on priority.

Answer Questions

Problem: The bug tracker is full of invalid reports and duplicates. You're losing security bugs in the pile.

When triaging bugs, you're asking yourself a few questions. How you handle the bug report depends on the answers.

- *Is this a bug?*   Not all issues in your bug tracker are bug reports. Users or other contributors will often file feature requests in the bug tracker as well. This is acceptable—even desirable—in most cases, but you'll still want to make sure you set the category appropriately. While you may accept bug fixes in passing, you may want to limit new features submissions to "trusted" developers or at least require additional planning work to discourage hasty contributions. If it's neither a bug nor a feature request, it might be a question or a support request. Mark it as such or—if your project uses a separate tool—direct the reporter to the right venue. Keep in mind that questions and support requests often highlight documentation bugs, so open a bug against your docs if that seems appropriate. Lastly, the report may be an unactionable rant or unrelated spam. You can close those without feeling bad.

- *Is it a duplicate?* If you're getting a feeling of *déjà vu*, the bug report may be a duplicate. Ideally, the reporter checked for existing issues that match theirs before submitting a new report. People don't always do that. But even if they did, they may have just missed it. If you spend a lot of time in the bug tracker, you can recognize duplicates when they come in and mark them as such. You'll probably miss some (see the sidebar at the end of this list) and that's okay. The more duplicates you catch, the more developer time you'll save.

- *Is it a security bug?* One of the foundational tenets of the free software movement is that users should control their computing. Security flaws violate that by giving someone else control of the computer in some way. These things happen, but you'll want to make sure you clearly mark them so that someone can fix them quickly. You want security bugs to stand out to developers.

- *Is it filed in the right place?* Users don't always know where the problem lies; they know how they experience it. The larger and more complex your project is, the more likely it is that the bug report will be misfiled initially. A Fedora kernel maintainer once told me that the kernel component seems to be the starting point for any bugs that happen during the boot process because there are so many moving parts and it's hard for most people to tell where the actual failure happens. The bug might not even be in your software to begin with—it could be in an upstream project. In that case, you might close your report and direct the user upstream or act as a bug concierge and file the report for them. Regardless, part of bug triage is to attempt to get the report into the right place using your deeper knowledge of the project. Of course, the bug report may still get passed around a few times before it gets fixed.

- *Is it reproducible?* You don't necessarily need to reproduce every bug yourself, but you should make sure that the report contains the information needed to reproduce it. If it doesn't, ask the reporter to provide what's missing. After a few weeks pass with no reply, you can choose to close the bug.

How Many Duplicates Do You Have?

Bear in mind that the number of bug reports marked as duplicate isn't the same concept as the number of duplicate bug reports. In theory, a project with a small number of bugs will have relatively few duplicates because it's very easy to check before filing a new report. As the number of bugs increases, you may expect the number of duplicates to increase proportionally, especially as you get into very large numbers because it becomes more difficult to find duplicates.

When I looked at the duplicate percentages for Fedora Linux bug reports,[a] I saw a different picture. Once a component had enough bugs to rise out of the "noise," the percentage of duplicate bugs held fairly steady, as expected. But the components with the most bugs saw a *decrease* in the duplicate percentage.

The challenge users face when trying to find existing bug reports also applies to project contributors. When a project has several thousand bug reports, it's unlikely that anyone can look at a new report and say "ah yes, this is probably a duplicate of bug 12345." So don't worry about missing some duplicates. But be wary of making decisions based on reports marked duplicate when you're actually thinking of duplicate bugs.

a. https://communityblog.fedoraproject.org/exploring-our-bugs-part-1-the-basics/

Ideally, you answer all of the questions in this section when the bug is filed before any real debugging work begins. But partial triage is better than no triage, and the answers may change as the report is investigated further.

Create a Triage Process

Problem: There's no coordinated process for triaging bugs. Some get triaged right away. Some don't get triaged at all. Some get triaged twice.

Once the questions in the previous section are answered, the bug report is appropriately marked as triaged. Then you send it off to the developers to get fixed. But how did you answer those questions in the first place?

This is one of the most challenging aspects you'll face as a program manager in an open source project. It is labor-intensive work that doesn't appeal to most people, so it scales very poorly. Small projects probably don't have enough bugs to need a process. Large projects have too many bug reports to reliably triage each one. This section describes a process that can work for the middle-sized projects, but don't feel bad if you find you end up triaging bugs on an *ad hoc* basis.

First, you must assemble a triage team. Bug triage is difficult, often thankless work. Don't be surprised if volunteers are scarce. Not just any volunteers will do. Triagers need a moderate understanding of how the project works at a technical level. If the project has multiple components, they need to know what each one does and doesn't do so they can sort it into the right pile. But again, some triage is better than no triage. If you can get someone to do basic categorization and check that the report contains the required information, that's a big help. Over time, if they stick around, they'll learn how the pieces fit together.

Next, let's figure out how the team will interact. Although doing a live triage meeting is a great way to share knowledge, it's slow and not particularly accessible for a distributed volunteer team. Consider pairing newcomers with an experienced person for a brief period to learn the ropes, but after that, your triagers will work mostly independently. Since, unlike medical triage, they're not making life or death decisions, it's okay for them to be fast and wrong. But they should have a channel to communicate with each other to ask questions or get help on something that truly stumps them. Regular meetings to discuss patterns, ask questions, and ask for a second opinion provide the team with an opportunity to grow.

Of course, there has to be some way to get the new bug reports to the triage team, so let's look at a few options. The simplest way is to have new reports automatically assigned to the team. Triagers can pick bugs out of the team's queue and assign them to the right place (or leave them unassigned) once the bug report is ready. The downside is that if the triage team doesn't get to a bug report, it'll sit there and not get fixed. An alternative is to have a report that lists the new, untriaged bugs and have triagers work from that. This means if a developer starts working on a bug before the triage team gets to it, they do their own triage. That's fine, since the point is to help get the bugs fixed, not win a turf war. When someone triages the bug report, they apply a label (however your bug tracker implements this) to indicate that it's done.

Although the word triage comes from the French word for sorting, the "triage" spelling implies that it'll age you three times as fast. That's a reasonable interpretation. Do what you can to recognize and reward your triage team for the work they do. And expect to see a lot of turnover on the team.

Prioritize Bugs

Problem: No one is sure which bugs are the most important. Trivial bugs get fixed long before serious bugs.

The priority of a bug—in which order it gets fixed—is generally up to the person working on it. People are contributing on a volunteer basis; you can't dictate priorities to them. By and large, they'll work on the bugs that they think are important, and their own interests and abilities are factors in that assessment. But most developers understand that being in a community means taking the community's priorities into account. That means the community has some say in what bugs are most important. So let's develop a framework for evaluating a bug's priority from the community's perspective, not the individual's.

Ask Questions

Problem: Each contributor prioritizes differently. There's no consistency in priorities, which frustrates contributors and users alike.

As with triage, you ask a set of questions to set a bug's priority. But sometimes questions need technical investigation of the bug before they can be answered. And while basic triage mostly involves objective decisions about a bug report, you make subjective decisions for prioritization. Ask the following questions when you're evaluating a bug's priority:

- *Can physical harm result from this bug?* We often talk about the Internet like it's separate from "real life." This is wrong. The software your project produces can be physically harmful. For example, a poorly secured web application might leak the mailing address of a user. Software that controls hardware could cause the device to draw too much current and start a fire. Thankfully these cases are rare, but you must be aware.

- *Does this bug cause data loss or corruption?* Yes, backups are important. No, most people don't have a sufficiently robust backup scheme in place. A bug that causes data loss can be enough to scare users away forever. If it happens in a business environment, it could cost your user real money. If it happens at home, it could result in the loss of irreplaceable mementos—pictures from grandma's 90th birthday party or a video of a baby's first steps.

- *Does this bug allow unauthorized access?* Bugs that allow someone to access—or worse, modify—systems or data they're not supposed to are bad. Even if no physical harm results, it could lead to a loss of data. A system may be used to send a harassing, fraudulent, or otherwise impermissible message. It could incur financial costs, or cause harm to someone's reputation.

- *Is accessibility reduced by the bug?* Software is only useful to the degree that people can use it. If a bug breaks accessibility features, that makes it less useful. This might include screen reader functionality or the ability to resize text. If a GUI or website can't be used without a mouse, that's an accessibility bug, too.

- *Is the default configuration affected?* Most people won't deviate far from the default configuration. It represents your project's opinionated view on how the software should work. So if there's a bug in the default, that's more important than a bug in a custom configuration, all other things being equal. If nothing else, a bug in the default configuration is likely to affect a much larger portion of the user base.

- *Do you not have a reasonable work-around?* If there's a way to avoid the bug, or at least to mitigate the harm, then it might go further down the priority list. "Reasonable" is doing a lot of work here. The work-around has to be something that a typical user can do easily and without significant loss of functionality.

- *Does the bug affect all platforms?* In an ideal world, it doesn't matter which hardware and operating system are in use. A bug is a bug. But in the real world, not all platforms are the same. If the bug only occurs on Windows 3.1 running on an i286 processor, that's probably at the bottom of the pile. The important platforms vary from project to project. For Internet of Things projects, ARM processors are probably important, but mainframes are not.

- *Does the bug impact any key downstreams you have?* If users often or primarily get to your project's software by way of a downstream, this is a factor to consider. A bug that prevents a popular downstream project from working should move up the stack in most cases.

- *Is the bug embarrassing to your project's reputation?* Some bugs don't cause any particular harm, but they still make you look bad. Maybe you misspelled your project in the loading screen. Perhaps the insulting error message you put in as a placeholder didn't get removed before release. It could be related to functionality, too. If it takes 30 seconds for a WiFi connection to be available, that's functional but it's also annoying. They say that there's no such thing as bad publicity, but most of us would rather not have people saying bad things about us or our work.

One question remains that lends itself to a more objective decision (or at least a binary response). *Is this something the software must always (or never) do?* In other words, will you delay a release if you find a bug like this. We call this a "release blocker," which we'll cover in Set Release Criteria, on page 137. For now, let's assume that a bug report in your bug tracker is for a version that has already been released, so it's too late to be a blocker.

Rate the Priority

Problem: The priority of a bug isn't clearly and consistently communicated.

In the previous section, we asked a lot of questions, and all of them have answers that are more spectrum than binary. You're probably tempted right now to come up with a rating system and give each bug a score. Don't. Once you get beyond a few bugs per developer, it's less "a stack" and more "assorted piles." Remember that these decisions have a large amount of subjectivity, so attaching an exact value is lying to yourself. It's not even a particularly useful lie, as it'll cost a lot of your time to develop and refine the scoring system. Even then, a developer looking for a bug to fix might not fix the highest-scoring bug because they may not have the knowledge or skills to tackle that particular one.

So how do you put the answers to those questions into practice? Let's say a bug's priority falls on a low/medium/high scale. The questions are roughly in order of descending importance. The sooner you answer "yes" to a question, the higher the bug's priority. The more "yes" answers a bug gets, the higher its priority. So you might say that any bug that gets a "yes" to the first four questions previously discussed is a high priority, a "yes" to the remainder is medium, and all "no" answers is low. But if a medium priority bug has three or more "yes" answers, it's also a high-priority bug.

Another option is to have the priority be a binary state instead of a low/medium/high scale. With a binary state approach, a bug is either prioritized or not. A community member (whether user or contributor) nominates a bug and then a group evaluates it and makes a decision. The group can be fixed or variable (for example, "whoever shows up to the meeting this week"), but you should make sure to notify the assignee and the person who nominated it so they can weigh in on it. If you accept a bug as prioritized, that signals to the assignee that they should work on this one first. This can be particularly helpful if your project has a corporate sponsor or at least corporate contributors. You can use prioritized bugs to say "this is where your support is most valuable to the community at the moment."

You can also choose a mixed approach. You can have low/medium/high priority set by a developer or the triage team, but also have an extra tier of highest priority that requires an approval process. However you do it, you need to be aware of the proportion of high-priority bugs. If everything is the top priority, nothing is.

And of course, document the prioritization guidelines in your project's contributor documentation so that everyone can find them. If you have a triage team, and they're relatively skilled, they can set the priority at triage time. (Of course, with the understanding that it may be adjusted by whichever developer ends up working on it.) If you don't have a triage team, each developer can apply the agreed-upon prioritization guidelines as they work on a bug report.

Close Bugs

Problem: Bug reports remain open indefinitely. Some of them are old enough to drive a car.

In a perfect world, all of your bug reports will be closed because they were fixed. That doesn't actually happen. Even if you can fix every bug, not all of the reports you get will be valid. You need a way to handle invalid reports and the bugs you just can't (or won't) fix.

Closure Types

Problem: No one can tell at a glance what it means when a bug report is closed. Was it fixed?

Before we figure out the process for closing bug reports, we should decide on what closure means. At the most basic level, you can simply have bug reports be open or closed. But that doesn't convey much information to people who may look at the bugs later. And it makes the analysis you do in the next section much less useful.

So let's come up with some closure types to use. Think of this as a minimum level of granularity. As your bug report volume increases, it makes sense to add more granularity. Broadly speaking, you can start with three basic groupings of closure types: happy, sad for the user, and sad for the developer (although you don't want to use those names directly).

Happy closure types are bugs that get fixed. This can be a single "fixed" type. But you may want to expand into multiple types. If your project has multiple releases, particularly if they're developed in parallel, it helps to indicate that. You might have a "fixed: stable" for a bug that gets fixed in the stable branch (perhaps as part of a point release) and "fixed: development" for a bug that is fixed in the development stream.

"Sad user" closure types are for bug reports that represent actual bugs that aren't fixed. The user is sad because they took the time to file a bug report and you didn't fix it. At a minimum, this category includes at least two types.

- *Can't fix.* For whatever reason, this bug can't be fixed. Perhaps it is too difficult. Or maybe fixing it results in introducing a worse bug somewhere else. Sometimes developers come to rely on existing behavior, so while changing it is technically a bug fix, too much relies on the existing "wrong" behavior.

- *Won't fix.* This type is closely related to "can't fix." The difference here is you could fix it, but you're not going to. For example, the bug is reported against an end-of-life release. Another reason to mark a bug "won't fix" is because it's so low priority that it'll never get attention. You'd rather have it out of the way.

The "sad developer" closure types are for bugs that waste a developer's time. This may be because they're invalid, missing information, or something else. Of course, "sad developer" bug reports also make the users sad—they spent time on them, too.

- *Duplicate.* This is a valid bug report, but it already exists.

- *Invalid.* Something about this report makes it not a bug in some way. It might be that the reported behavior is what the software is supposed to do. Perhaps the bug isn't in your project but in an upstream library. Maybe it's not even a clear bug report—just an indecipherable rant about how terrible your project is. The "invalid" type is a leading candidate for splitting into multiple types as your bug tracker grows.

- *Can't reproduce.* Some reports aren't obviously invalid, but for whatever reason, they can't be reproduced by your team. They might be specific to a platform or environment. Sometimes you can figure it out and fix it anyway, but ultimately if you can't trigger the behavior, how do you know if you've fixed it?

- *Missing information.* This type represents reports that might be valid bugs, but information is missing. You don't want to immediately close a report with this type; give the reporter time to answer questions about missing information. But after a while, if the reporter hasn't provided the information needed, there's not much more you can do.

- *Spam.* If a site (such as your bug tracker) allows users to write content to it, eventually some spammer will post links on it. You should track spam separately from the "invalid" type because when you're doing analysis, you generally want to ignore these reports. Spam reports are almost always easy to distinguish and waste little of your time (but still *some* time, which is why they're in the "sad developer" category). Invalid reports submitted by an actual person might require a fair amount of back and forth before you reach that conclusion, so they represent actual time wasted.

I hear you asking "shouldn't most of those sad types just stay open instead?" Some argue that bugs that aren't fixed should remain open until they are, even if that means keeping them open indefinitely. That's certainly an option.

Leaving unfixed bugs open forever turns your bug tracker into an easy list of known issues, which can be helpful for people trying to decide whether or not to use your software. On the other hand, the more open bugs you have, the harder it can be to find the one you're looking for. It can lead to more duplicate reports because users can't find the existing report that matches the behavior they need fixed. The information can also grow stale. A bug may have been fixed later on as part of the fix for another bug, but the report never got closed.

For projects with a small number of reports, leaving valid bugs open can be fine. As you grow, you'll want to develop a strategy for pruning the open bugs.

Closure Process

Problem: No one knows when bugs will actually be closed.

How do you know when to close a bug? There's no objectively right answer, only the agreed practice of your community. As the program manager, you should have a strong opinion about this. Let's take a look at how to approach different types of closure.

The process for closing a fixed bug report is pretty simple: you close it! Actually, it's a little more complicated than that. When do you close it? You have two basic choices: close it when the fix is committed to the repository or close it when the release containing the fix is published. The first option is easier to manage, whereas the second one communicates the status more clearly. There's no right answer, but if you decide to go down the second route, you'll need to have a process to mark "release pending" bugs and close them when the release ships. In either case, the bug should contain the commit and release version for the fix. This will help future readers of the bug decide if the bug wasn't quite fixed after all. It's also a service to your users to include in the closure message what they should do if the fix doesn't actually fix it: do you want them to reopen the bug report? Create a new one? Something else?

The process for unfixed bugs will depend on the type you're using to close it. Let's start with a few easy ones.

When a release reaches end of life, close bug reports against that version. Ideally, you should comment a few weeks in advance to let the reporter (and developer) know that the bug is about to be closed and—if the behavior can be reproduced on a supported version—to update the report's version field.

Reports that are duplicate or spam can be closed as soon as you make that determination. The same goes for "can't fix," "can't reproduce," and invalid bugs. For those, the person closing the bug should explain why and invite the reporter to reopen or resubmit if something changes.

Some "won't fix" bugs can also be closed after deciding you won't ever fix them. But the majority will probably remain open for some time until the inevitability of the lack of a fix becomes obvious. The best approach is to figure out a time that marks the "we're just kidding ourselves" point and close bug reports that reach that age. One year is a reasonable time for smaller projects, up to perhaps three or four years for larger projects. You can either have automation that closes the reports when they reach the specified age or do it manually on a regular calendar basis. As with the end-of-life bugs, it's polite to give an advance notice and tell the reporter and developers what to do if the bug should be kept open.

The process for bugs that are missing information looks very similar to the "won't fix" process in the preceding paragraph, but with a shorter timeframe. One month is probably suitable in most cases. Like your contributors, your users may be participating in their free time, so you don't want to set the time too short. On the other hand, if they haven't replied after a month, it seems unlikely that they'll come back to it. Think about how long you take to reply to a question for a bug report you've submitted. What's the length of time where you know you'll never reply?

For all of your closure types, you should make sure the process is documented in a publicly visible way. People will complain about unfixed bugs being closed, but if the process is clear and consistent, that helps. In all cases, be honest about why a bug report is being closed before the bug is fixed. Explain the reasoning directly, but sincerely. If done right, this can be an opportunity for the reporter to get more involved in the project.

Analyze Bugs

Problem: You don't know what your bugs mean. Are you getting more or less with each release? Do reports get closed faster than in the past? What percentage of bugs are serious security issues?

Tracking your bug reports provides you with raw data, but that's not very interesting on its own. To get the most from it, you have to analyze that data. The tools and statistical methods for data analysis are beyond the scope of this book. For now, let's just say two things. One, you can answer a lot of questions with the basic descriptive statistics you learned in school. Two, a Jupyter notebook[2] and the pandas[3] data analysis toolkit are a great combination for shareable, interactive data analysis.

So why bother analyzing your bug reports? First, it lets you learn about your user community and how they actually use the software. Second, trends in the data can tell you what's going right—and wrong. Last, it challenges what you thought you knew. We'll go deeper on those first two in a moment, but first I'll share an example of challenging existing "knowledge."

For a long time, I believed that people always set the severity to "urgent" when filing a bug against Fedora Linux. I'd seen many occasions when an "urgent" bug turned out to be trivial. Surely that field can't be relied upon for anything. But then I looked at the severity for bug reports over a dozen releases, as shown in the figure on page 132.

Much to my surprise, only a small portion of reports was given "urgent" severity. In fact, the distribution was pretty close to what you'd expect from an objective categorization. Sure, there are cases where a bug report gets a higher severity than is warranted, but in aggregate, the field is still useful.

Learn Your Users

Problem: Your project's team has no idea what platforms people are using your software on.

What do you know about your user community? How do they use the software your project makes? Your bugs can give you some approximations.

Open source enthusiasts tend to be more privacy-conscious than the general population. The ability to inspect what a piece of code does is what brought some people to open source in the first place. So you're less likely to have

---

2. https://jupyter.org/
3. https://pandas.pydata.org/

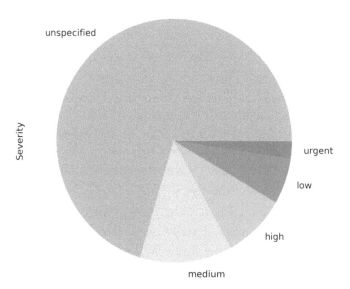

telemetry that automatically reports information back to the project. While users appreciate this, it means developers are often working in the dark, with only their own use cases to consider. Surveys are hard to do well (particularly ensuring the sample is representative) and only provide a snapshot in time. But your bug tracker can give you some rough clues!

If you have a lot of bugs filed on one platform and none on the other, you can reasonably assume the relative usage of each platform. Similarly, if your software has multiple components, you can often tell which ones get the most use because they have the most bug reports. Of course, this isn't perfect. For one, it assumes that the bugs are evenly distributed across platforms, components, and so on. It also fails to capture the nuances of *how* the software is being used. Is the presentation tool being used to create slide decks or posters? Both are valid uses, but they represent different needs.

Still, you have more information than you had before. While it's not perfect, it's at least defensible. Of course, the *contents* of the bug reports can often provide more information, but those are hard to process in bulk. If you're feeling particularly ambitious, you can add additional metadata fields to capture richer information, but that's generally not going to be worth the effort.

Examine Trends

Problem: You're not sure if things are getting better or worse—or if they're changing at all.

A snapshot in time does not always tell you much. The real insights come when you can look at trends over time. Are bug reports being closed faster? Does the rate of bug report increase match the rate of contributor increase? As with using bug data as a user survey proxy, you can't always draw iron-clad conclusions. But you can get a good idea of how things are going and—critically—see if your perceptions match reality.

To start, you probably want to "bucketize" your bug reports. This means grouping them by some common value. If you have regular releases, the release version is a good option. If not, or if you've only had a few releases, you might bin them by date (by month or quarter, most likely). The idea here is that open source projects have irregular participation, so grouping the bugs into logical categories gets rid of some of the natural noise in the data.

Releases Don't Strictly Equal Time

 One thing to be aware of when you use release version buckets is that the buckets don't strictly equal time in most cases. If you support releases in parallel, a bug report filed more recently against an older version will appear older in your analysis. For example, Fedora Linux releases have a life span of approximately 13 months so a bug filed at the beginning of the F35 cycle may be older than a bug filed at the end of the F34 cycle. For most projects, this is probably fine. If your project is providing five years of support for a release, that may require some changes. You might consider using the life cycle phases you set on page 73 or the year the report was filed to provide some more granular results.

Buckets don't have to be time-based, though. You can also group your reports by things like bug severity or components. This allows you to make comparisons across different parts of the project. If you're looking for an understanding of usage, as in the previous subsection, this is a good way to get it. You can even bucket in two dimensions. For example, you can look at the distribution of bug severity separately for each release.

Don't Use Assignees as Buckets

You'll be tempted to consider using the individual assignees as buckets when analyzing bug reports. That's a bad idea. First, you don't want to be seen as shaming anyone, and by comparing your contributors to each other, you're only inviting competition and gaming. People will try to race to the top of the leaderboard and will use whatever tricks they can to improve their scores. Those who have low scores will be demoralized and might decide that they have better places where they can volunteer their time. Second, the assignee value isn't particularly reliable. A bug is often solved by several people. Sometimes the nominal assignee never even touches the report.

Using assignees is valuable in one way. It's not as a bucket but as a count. Counting the number of unique assignees can be a rough proxy for the size of the community providing user support. The caveats in the previous paragraph still apply, but they can at least give you something to work with. If the bug reports are increasing faster than the assignees, that may be an indication that you need to grow your contributor community.

After you have your buckets, it's time to decide what trends to examine. What is it that you want to know?

Let's keep the focus on trends that would cause the community to change its behavior. Knowing that the number of unique bug reporters is increasing each release gives you a good clue that your user base is growing, but it won't change your development practices. On the other hand, if you see that the number of urgent bugs is doubling every release, that should cause you to reexamine your QA (or triage) practices.

In some cases, the bug tracker keeps you from answering the questions you want to ask. In Fedora Linux, it's common for a bug report to be re-assigned to a different component a few times. But how many times? We use Bugzilla as our tracker, but it doesn't provide that information easily. I would have to query the history of each bug to get a count, and with dozens of releases each with ten thousand or so bugs, that's a lot of API calls to make. So I do without it.

As you're looking at your trends, consider what's the most meaningful way to represent them. What's more meaningful to your question: a raw number or a percentage? An increase in urgent bugs from 10 to 100 between releases sounds big, but if the total bug count goes from 100 to 10,000, the *percentage* drops from 10% to 1%. Both of those values are true, but only one of them tells the story correctly. In general, if you're talking about the size of a category (for example, the severity or closure type), you'll want to use a percentage. The exception to that is if there's a direct relationship between a count and the effort required. For example, if each urgent bug report requires an analysis from your one security expert, then going from 10 to 100 is a big deal for the security expert, even if the percentage drops.

Let's also think about what to exclude. When do you care about spam entries? Only when you're asking "how much spam do we get?" For every other question, set those aside. Similarly, you'll often want to exclude duplicates from your calculations. Think about whether the number of people reporting the same bug is important to your question. If it's not, exclude duplicates.

Beware of Average Distorters

Excluding bug reports that distract from the question at hand is particularly important when you're asking questions like "how quickly are we resolving bugs?" Duplicate, spam, and invalid bug reports tend to be closed very quickly. If you include them, you artificially lower your average. While this might make you feel good, it gives you the wrong answer.

After you have sliced and diced your data to see the trends, the last step is to *see* the trends. You can do this in text or graphs. The best choice will almost always be graphs. A line chart will suit your needs well in many cases. That's great for representing questions like "how many bugs were reported over time?" or "how has our median closure time changed?" For data with a large spread, a box plot can show that well. The box plot on page 136 shows the mean time to resolution for the Fedora Linux bugs that were closed with a "happy" closure type. You can see that there are many outliers, but it shows that the general trend is for a shorter time to resolution and a smaller spread.

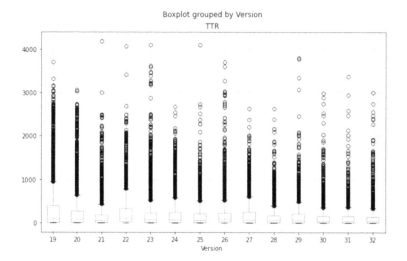

Retrospective

You now understand how the bug tracker is a program manager's most powerful tool for understanding the present and predicting the future. Your bug tracker does not just tell you about your software—it tells you about your contributors and your users, too. By building a system to appropriately triage your bugs, you can make sure the most important bugs are getting fixed. And now that you know what to track, you can see how the process changes you make impact the bug reports. In the next chapter, we'll continue to talk about a specific kind of bug: release blockers.

## CHAPTER 11

Ship the Release

Congratulations! You made it to the end of the release cycle, and now it's time to ship the release. Well, once you do a few more things. This chapter covers the run-up to pushing the big, red "release now" button. As the program manager, you're probably not the one to actually press the button, but you'll be the one to make sure the process goes smoothly.

Set Release Criteria

Problem: You don't know when the release is ready to ship.

If you're waiting until all of the (known) bugs are fixed before you ship the release, you're going to need a very comfortable chair. The only way to produce meaningful software without any (known) bugs is to avoid testing. Since that seems like a recipe for disaster, we have to come up with another approach. Let's figure out which bugs are acceptable and which aren't.

We can start by turning to our bug tracker and looking at all of the bugs in the prerelease version. For each one, we ask ourselves "is it okay to ship the release with this bug?" This involves a few difficulties. First, debating each bug will take a long time. Not everyone will agree on whether the behavior is acceptable, and individuals may not be consistent in their definition of "acceptable" from bug to bug. This process is also unpredictable. Developers won't be able to tell which bugs are likely to be considered release-blocking and may put their efforts into the wrong bugs, delaying the release.

The better approach is to define a set of *release criteria*—the behaviors the software must (or mustn't) have to be released.

Define the Criteria

Problem: You don't know where to start with release criteria.

Writing release criteria from scratch is hard, so I suggest borrowing from another project. For example, the Fedora Linux release criteria[1] have had more than a decade of polish. As with all things open source, you might as well build on the work of others. Even if you don't take any of the criteria directly, you'll be inspired by what you see.

But let's assume you'll have to write at least *some* criteria from scratch. How can you do that? The easiest way to start is to think of the obvious criteria. You don't want to delete the user's data willy-nilly right? So let's put down "Must not delete data unless explicitly instructed to by the user." Congratulations! You just wrote your first release criterion.

How you fill out the rest of the criteria is very project-dependent. A Linux distribution should include "the system must successfully boot," but a web browser doesn't need to worry about that. Go through the major features of your software. What are the things it absolutely must do? Write those down, too. Try to think about it from the user's perspective. If you're developing a blogging platform, you might think the ability to post is critical. It is. But for your users, the ability to add themes or otherwise customize the site is as important—that's what makes it *their* site. So you'd want to include something like "user-selected themes must be applied correctly."

At this point, you're probably finding yourself adding a lot of criteria to the list. Be careful with that. Remember how we agreed you can't wait until there are zero bugs? If everything your software can do is a release criterion, you're going to have a hard time ever getting a release out. As with all things program management, you have to strike the right balance. This is about deciding which types of bugs you can tolerate and which you can't.

So how do you decide what you can't tolerate? Think back to the questions we asked when prioritizing bugs on page 124. Bugs that can result in physical harm, data loss, or unauthorized access are ones you don't want to ship with the release in the first place. Write release criteria that cover those cases.

Next, focus on cases where it would be hard to deliver a fix. These days, most software can be updated pretty easily after the fact, so your users aren't forever stuck with bugs that ship in the initial release. But if the bug happens in installer media—like ISO images or software preinstalled on IoT devices—once the bug is out, it'll be harder to get the fix to everyone. You may want to block the release on bugs that impact the preinstall or the first-use experience even

---

1.   https://fedoraproject.org/wiki/Basic_Release_Criteria

if you can fix them in an update later. After all, you don't get a second chance to make a first impression.

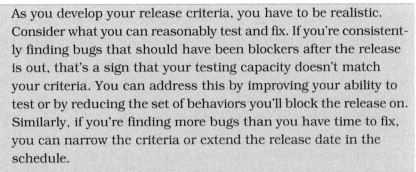

Be Realistic

As you develop your release criteria, you have to be realistic. Consider what you can reasonably test and fix. If you're consistently finding bugs that should have been blockers after the release is out, that's a sign that your testing capacity doesn't match your criteria. You can address this by improving your ability to test or by reducing the set of behaviors you'll block the release on. Similarly, if you're finding more bugs than you have time to fix, you can narrow the criteria or extend the release date in the schedule.

The release criteria reflect your commitment to both your contributor community and your users. When you're consistently making exceptions or trying to find creative interpretations so you can make a case to finally ship the release, that's a clear indication of a mismatch between the criteria and reality. You owe it to the community to keep these aligned. Otherwise, you're just pretending.

Write Criteria

Problem: You're unsure how to write the criteria effectively.

Now that we know what we need the release to do, we have to write it down. This isn't as easy as it sounds. Yes, you simply take the thoughts and turn them into words. But the words matter.

You want the focus to be on whether or not a bug violates a particular release criterion, not on the meaning of the criterion. This means the wording needs to be as specific and objective as you can make it. For example, "the installer must be able to use HTTP, HTTPS, and NFS repositories as package sources" is better than "the installer must be able to use network repositories as package sources" because it explicitly identifies the protocols. The installer may also include support for FTP and gopher, but you won't block the release on those because they're not a part of that criterion. Similarly, "the built package must be no larger than 2 gigabytes" is better than "the built package must fit on a USB drive" or "the built package must not be too large." "Too large" is very ambiguous and USB drives come in a range of sizes.

Avoid vague words like "work." You're using the release criteria to define what "work" means for your project. Instead of saying "the plugin manager must work," be specific about what the plugin manager must do. Does it have to successfully install plugins from a local source? From a network source? Does it have to successfully remove plugins? Does that mean removing any local configuration or should that be left in case the user decides to reinstall later?

Of course, not everything can be written with inarguable certainty. Sometimes you need to be a little vague. If you say "the application must reach the home page within two seconds of launch," that's good and specific. But what if that's only possible on top-of-the-line hardware? Do you want to block the release if someone is running the application on their decade-old laptop or an underpowered single-board computer? In this case, you might want to use a mushy phrase like "...within a reasonable time." What's "reasonable"? You can provide some (nonbinding) benchmarks to help the community come to a shared definition.

The shared definition is the tricky part. It's not enough that you understand what you meant when you wrote a particular criterion. People who have never met you need to understand what you meant, too. This is why specific wording is the better choice when possible. When it's not possible, try to give the reader a frame of reference with benchmarks, orders of magnitude, or explanatory notes.

The Case for a Totally Vague Release Criterion

In this section, we've emphasized the need for clear and objective criteria. But there's also a place for a vague "this is just too bad to release" criterion. When there's a bug that will severely damage your initial reviews, you might want to consider it a release-blocker. Essentially, it's more of a marketing decision at this point than a QA decision.

How do you decide? Use what I call "the Potter Stewart rule." In *Jacobellis v. Ohio*, United States Supreme Court Justice Potter Stewart avoided giving a specific definition of "hard-core pornography," saying instead "perhaps I could never succeed in intelligibly [defining the term]. But I know it when I see it."[a] You can't define it ahead of time, but when a bug pops up, you know it.

The challenge is that you want to keep this for emergency use only. Otherwise, you slowly begin applying it to more and more bugs until it loses all meaning. Eventually, you lose all of the benefits of having release criteria. If you choose to allow for "Potter Stewart bugs," have a clear and separate process for them, like requiring a vote by the project's governing body.

---

a.   https://en.wikipedia.org/wiki/Jacobellis_v._Ohio

After you have all the wording written down, there's one more step: organize the criteria. This is entirely optional, but you'll find it makes life easier—especially as your criteria become more numerous. Start by broadly categorizing the criteria. Put all of the installation-related criteria under an "Installation" header, the theming criteria under a "Themes" header, and so on. As an added bonus, assign numbers to each one. It's much easier to refer to "criterion 3b" than to "printing must work on at least one printer available to those performing validation testing."

Change Criteria

Problem: You're missing a criterion, or one has become outdated.

You've figured out by now that your work is never done. At some point, you'll need to modify your release criteria. Maybe you discovered something that absolutely should block the release, but it got overlooked when you were doing the first draft. Perhaps a feature has been added or modified in a way that changes an existing criterion or requires a new one. Or it could be that your users' expectations have shifted. Whatever the reason, don't be surprised when you need to change your criteria.

Changing the criteria looks a lot like writing the initial criteria. The main difference is in the process. Changes to release criteria tend to pop up in the heavy testing before a release. This is natural. As you get into testing, you find the things that don't match what you want.

You'll be tempted to make the changes immediately. That's not necessarily bad, but you need to be deliberate about it. As you've read, effective program management is all about finding the right balance. In this case, it's the balance between having the criteria be as correct as possible and giving developers a predictable target. If you keep making last-minute changes to the release criteria, the community will lose trust in the process.

When modifying the criteria, especially late in the schedule, ask if the modification can wait until the next release. This prevents last-minute fire drills to fix issues that weren't a problem a few days ago. Sometimes, of course, you don't want to ship a particular bug. That's okay, but the rarer you can make the last-minute changes, the better the process will work. With changes due to planned features, of course, you can include that as part of the feature proposal template on page 100.

Freeze the Code

Problem: The QA team is having trouble verifying the behavior because the code base keeps changing.

It's much easier to inspect something that's holding still. This is true for code, too. As the release approaches, the testing effort shifts from verifying individual changes to looking at the product as a whole. The QA team needs to have a relatively stable code base to test so they can be sure the release criteria are met. If a test was performed yesterday but the code changes today, how can we be sure it still works without rerunning all of the tests?

A code freeze provides an unmoving code base for testing. Some projects use the term "merge window" instead, which is essentially the time when a freeze isn't in effect. In either case, the effect is the same: there's a time when developers make minimal changes, usually to fix bugs. This allows testers to be confident that test status won't change unexpectedly.

Depending on the size of your project, you might not want *all* bug fixes to land during a freeze. Bug fixes sometimes result in new bugs, which can defeat the entire point of the freeze. You want to fix bugs that violate the release criteria, of course, but less important bugs might need to wait. In large or particularly complex projects, you might choose to have a separate freeze exception process. You can grant freeze exceptions to permit fixes for bugs that are significant but don't rise to the level of blocking the release.

How long should the freezes last? We skipped that part when building the release schedule on page 88, so let's discuss it now that we have a better understanding. There are two competing interests to balance. Longer freezes give QA more time to test. Shorter freezes mean fewer changes queue up to land as soon as the code thaws, which makes the immediate postfreeze time less tumultuous. As a starting point, take the amount of time that it takes the testing team to verify all of the release criteria and triple it. This allows for the uncertainty of volunteer availability and also gives some space to revalidate after blocking bugs get fixed. With each release, you can evaluate how the freeze went and shorten or extend it as appropriate for the next time.

Produce Release Candidates

Problem: You don't know what code to release.

A release candidate is exactly what it sounds like: the code that's a candidate for release. If a release candidate passes, has no release-blocking bugs, and is approved for release, that's what you ship. Ideally, you ship that build. If you generate a new build after approving the release candidate, it's possible that the actual release differs in subtle but important ways.

Unlike in politics, you're not choosing from two or more candidates. You might end up producing multiple release candidates, but they are done in series. Once RC2 is built, RC1 is no longer a viable release candidate. You build one release candidate at a time until you have one that is ready to ship.

You can take two general approaches to produce release candidates. Let's call them "defined" and "ad hoc." The defined approach plans for several release candidates on scheduled dates. This bakes in the assumption that you'll need to do several rounds of bug fixes. Python is a notable user of this approach. Each release schedule (for example, Python 3.11[2]) includes two release candidates roughly a month apart, with a final release planned about a month after the second release candidate. This works well for large projects, particularly ones that are foundational to so many others like Python.

The ad hoc approach calls for producing a release candidate when you think the code is ready. This isn't to say that you've fixed every bug in the code base, but that the testing you've been doing along the way suggests the release candidate will pass. In this approach, you start producing release candidates as soon as you think you're ready. In general, you'll want to require the release candidate to exist a minimum time before your go/no-go decision to permit completion of the validation tests. Fedora uses this approach. A release candidate is produced once all of the blocking bugs have a potential fix. If validation tests pass, the candidate moves forward. If not, the bugs are fixed and another release candidate is generated. The advantage of the ad hoc approach is that you have a lot of flexibility. The disadvantage is that you'll find yourself tempted to keep shortening the window between producing the release candidate and deciding its fate.

The other question to consider in regard to release candidates is the audience. You can either treat the release candidate as an "internal" deliverable only tested by your core QA group or you can treat it as an "external" deliverable that you announce to the community. There's no right or wrong answer. In part, it depends on the size of your QA team and the required testing environment. The larger your team or more specialized the testing environment is (for example, if specific hardware is required), the less you benefit from externalizing the release candidate. And there's effort involved in sharing the information about the release candidate and helping inexperienced testers with their testing and reporting. Everything is public in an open source project,

---

2.   https://www.python.org/dev/peps/pep-0664/

though, so even if you're largely targeting your release candidate inward, you can't keep it secret.

Determine Readiness

Problem: You don't know if the team is ready to release.

It's not enough for the software to be ready. Your team needs to be ready, too. What good is making the code available if no one hears about it, or knows where to find it? What "ready" means can vary from project to project, but let's look at a few areas that are likely to come up.

- *Release announcement.* Do you have one written? Whether you send it via email, blog post, press release, or anything else, the release announcement is how most people find out about the release.

- *Website.* For many projects, the website is how users find and download the new version. If the website needs to be updated to point to the new release (or use new screenshots), those need to be done before you can call it ready.

- *Documentation.* Do you have release notes ready? Has all of the documentation been verified and updated? Users will be excited to try out the new features, so you need to have documentation ready to help them.

- *Marketing.* This can include social media posts queued up but also any flyers you hand out or web ads you run. It could also include funding and organizing release parties and other local events. You might also send "talking points" to contributors so they know what to highlight when talking about the release.

- *Translations.* Everything we've discussed so far can be translated and localized. If that's something your project does, you'll want that to be ready for the release.

- *Infrastructure.* Does your website get a big spike in traffic in the first week a release is out? If so, you'll want to make sure the infrastructure is ready for the increased load. If you use a network of mirrors to distribute the software, you'll want to make sure the artifacts have been copied to all of the mirrors.

This list isn't comprehensive. You'll likely think of additional tasks or areas that apply to your specific project, but it gives us a good starting point to work from.

Remember how you've read over and over again that program management is all about finding the balance? Well, it's about one other thing, too: avoiding surprises. The release day is the worst time to find out something isn't ready.

A few ways are available for you to can ensure everything is ready ahead of time. The first is to put the critical tasks on your release schedule and follow up to make sure they're completed. You can also conduct a meeting in advance of the release day to coordinate between the different teams. Or if you prefer an asynchronous approach, you can have representatives of each area update a dashboard with their status. Of course, passively watching each area and keeping an eye on their progress is also an option. However you accomplish it, the goal is to know what's ready and what tasks could use help.

Make the Decision

Problem: You think you're ready to release, but you don't know how to be sure.

Now that we've spent most of the chapter setting up the framework for knowing when the code and the team are ready, let's put that to use. If you've been paying close attention to the project in the run-up to the release decision, the decision should be no surprise. You already know where everything stands. But sometimes the decision requires a judgment call, so let's figure out how to do that.

Set Requirements

Problem: You don't know how to apply the readiness frameworks.

Making the decision sounds simple: if the code and the team are both ready, you release. But it's not that simple. Sometimes a blocker bug can be hard to fix. Or some groups in the project aren't ready yet. These things happen. You can't wait until everything is perfect, or else you'll never release it. So you have to figure out how to get as close as you can.

The first requirement is that all of the release-blocking bugs are fixed. Difficulty: not all bugs can be fixed in a reasonable timeframe. Sometimes that means waiving blocker bugs and releasing anyway. You might choose to waive a blocker for a variety of reasons such as, it's too difficult to fix, it only affects a small set of use cases, or it's marginal and was only found the night before release. Whatever the reason, treat all of your blockers as valid until it's time to make the final decision. The decision to waive a blocking bug isn't one to make lightly. You don't want to have waiving be automatic. Instead, explicitly decide whether or not to waive for each outstanding blocker bug.

To ensure you've caught all of the blockers in the first place, you might also choose to require specific tests to be run. These can be manual or automatic tests, but the release candidate should pass them one way or another. Of course, you can test more than the required set. The point is to have confidence in what you ship because you know it passed the tests. You don't want to require passing every test—choose the most important ones (like the tests that cover your release criteria).

Finally, you need to decide what's the minimum acceptable team readiness. Community-driven projects don't always have stable contributions—when people are volunteering, sometimes they need to prioritize other parts of their lives. So you might find that something is left undone come release time. Can you release if the translations aren't completed? What if the marketing material isn't updated? This isn't about deciding what's unimportant in the project. The question is "what can we live without if everything else is ready?"

For all of these requirements, it's best if you write them down *before* the release day. This way everyone knows what to expect. You don't want to lose credibility because people think you're making up the rules to suit the decision you wanted to make.

Make the Go or No-Go Decision

Problem: You don't have a process for making the decision.

Okay, you have your requirements in hand. You know the state of the code. You know which teams are ready. Now—finally—it's time to decide whether or not to ship the release.

You can choose to make the decision synchronously or asynchronously. The synchronous approach involves holding a go/no-go meeting. You review the requirements and verify that everything is ready. If something isn't ready—or the readiness is uncertain—you can have an immediate discussion and then make the decision.

Of course, meetings can be hard to schedule. They'll end up excluding people who can't be available at the specified time. Instead, you can choose to have a voting system (it doesn't have to be fancy), where updates are provided over the course of a day or two. If everyone reports "go," then you ship. This adds delay, of course. If something needs to be discussed, the conversation takes longer. Choose the method that works best for your community.

Whichever approach you take, you should announce the decision once it's made. If it takes time to stage the content out to mirrors or otherwise get it ready, you can start that process once "go" is declared. If the release is "no-go," announce that, along with why it's that way and the next target release date.

Retrospective

Congratulations! You made it to the end of the release cycle and now it's time to ship the release. No, I really mean it this time. You set up the frameworks to determine when the code and the team are ready. You decided to ship the release. Now it's in the hands of your users. Your hard work has paid off.

Now that the release is out the door, take some time to reflect on how things went. What could you—both "you" as in "my dear reader" and "you" as in "the contributor community"—have done better? What got overlooked or ignored? Take your plans and tweak them for the next time. And don't forget to celebrate the things that went well. You saw all of the flaws and missteps, but most people only see the successful release.

Well, here we are at the end of the book. You've come a long way in eleven chapters. You have the knowledge you need to start getting your ducks in a row. The rest will come with practice, experimentation, and the occasional failure. But you'll be managing your program with intent, and that's a great start.

Choose Your Tools

Your success as a program manager isn't based on your charm and good looks. The right tools are crucial to help you be effective and efficient. So which tools are the right ones? There's no simple answer. As in the rest of this book, it depends on your specific needs and those of your community.

In this appendix, we'll explore some considerations to help you make the right choice. You'll be asked to think about what matters, both practically and philosophically. But we'll generally steer clear of discussing specific tools. Software changes quickly, as you know all too well, and I didn't want to cover software that could be out of date by the time you read this book. For the discussion of specific tools, read my Duck Alignment Academy blog.[1]

Identify Your Requirements

If you've ever procured software for work, this section will seem familiar to you. Not all software is alike, so you have to figure out what specifically you want. This means identifying your requirements.

Functional Requirements

The first thing to consider when selecting a tool is what you need it to do. This may seem obvious, but too often the requirements are assumed. Documenting the functional requirements gives you an easy way to compare your options. Sharing the requirements with the community allows you to get input from different perspectives you might have missed.

The word "functional" is important here. Focus on what you want the tool to do, not on the attributes you want it to have. For a git forge, you might include "allow users outside the core developer team to submit proposed code

---

1.   https://duckalignment.academy/tag/tools/

changes," but you wouldn't say "proposed code changes should be called 'pull requests'."

Collect the must-have and nice-to-have features, written as tersely as possible. You'll find using the terms "must" and "should" as defined in RFC 2119[2] helpful in separating must- and nice-to-have requirements. Once you have the requirements documented, you can use a spreadsheet to provide a ready comparison between your choices. This has the added bonus of being able to assign a different relative weight to some of the nice-to-have features.

We need to think about a few general questions for all tools before we start looking at tool-specific questions later in this appendix.

- *What authentication systems does the tool support?* If your project has an in-house authentication system, can you use that in this tool? Does it allow other external identity providers (for example, popular git forges and social networks) or are accounts strictly local?

- *Does it provide an API?* Since you will likely be writing "glue" to connect the tools you pick in a way that fits your workflow, you will want an easy way to export and import data. Give the tool bonus points if it offers a library for your programming language of choice, but a REST API can go a long way.

Now that you have your functional requirements defined, you can look at other attributes to narrow the field.

Open Source

The next question you should ask yourself is: "does the tool need to be open source?" Communities have varying opinions on this question. In some communities, any tool that isn't open source is unacceptable. Other communities don't particularly care.

If you're reading this book, you don't need to be told the benefits of open source software. You're producing it, after all! But for some communities, *producing* open source software doesn't require exclusively *using* open source software. They may prefer open source but are willing to accept the use of proprietary solutions when the open source alternatives don't meet the functional needs.

These days, most projects will use at least some proprietary (such as GitHub) or "open core" (such as GitLab) tools. There's no objectively "right" position

---

2.   https://www.ietf.org/rfc/rfc2119.txt

to take. You have to make sure the tool you select matches the philosophy of your community or else they won't use it.

Hosting

Next, you need to ask yourself if the tool needs to be self-hosted or if you can use a Software-as-a-Service (SaaS) offering. This question is often related to the previous one. If you select a proprietary tool, it's probably going to be SaaS unless you pay a lot of money. But open source and open core tools will often have a SaaS offering in addition to the installable version. Communities often prefer running their own tools to keep control over their infrastructure and data. But this requires hardware and the time and expertise of system administrators. Free software often ends up being "free as in puppy."[3]

Larger projects with reliable funding are often better positioned to run their own infrastructure. They sometimes scale beyond what the free tier of a SaaS offering allows. And larger projects often have larger and more complex infrastructure needs, which enable some of the cost to be spread across services. Still, the time your contributors spend keeping the infrastructure running is time they're not spending producing what the project is intended to produce, so be careful about what you choose to run yourself. If you have the funds, a paid tier of an open source SaaS tool can be a good compromise: you're not running the tool yourself, and you're funding another project to keep their work going.

Development

One way to avoid some of these questions is to write the software yourself. This way, it'll do exactly what you want in exactly the way you want it to. You can choose the license that is most perfectly aligned with your community's values. And you can host it yourself or on any cloud service. This is a tempting option.

It's also a trap. Writing your own tooling should be reserved for exceptional cases. If there's nothing already in existence that reasonably meets your needs, then you can write your own. But the time your community spends writing tooling is time not spent developing the project you're ostensibly working on. And in many cases, the resulting tool will be inferior to what you could have gotten elsewhere. If your community is building an installable solitaire game, do you have the expertise available to build a secure web service for your build system? Maybe, but maybe not.

---

3. https://opensource.com/article/17/2/hidden-costs-free-software

Of course, no tool is going to be perfect, so you may need to put *some* development work into whatever you select. Ideally, this will be an open source project used by several other communities so that you can all collaborate together. Even if the upstream doesn't want to add the features you need, you can maintain a fork with those changes. It's not zero effort, but it at least saves you on reimplementing the parts that already exist. Look at peer projects. What tools are they happy with? If no one is happy with their tools, maybe you can join forces to create something you'll all be happy with. Better yet, maybe you can join forces to improve what already exists.

Pick Your Tools

While you can apply some requirements to any tools (for example, you will want to require any web-based tool to use HTTPS), other requirements are going to be tool-specific. The remainder of this appendix discusses some key tools you will want to add to your toolbox and some considerations when picking them.

One thing to note before we start looking at tool types: there's not a one-to-one mapping. You can sometimes use the same tool for multiple purposes. Using the back tracker as a ticket system is common, and many bug tracking tools these days include kanban-like functionality. A multipurpose tool may not always be the best fit for any single role, but it's sometimes worth having slightly worse functionality in a single place.

Your smartphone is a good example. It doesn't take pictures as well as a single-lens reflex camera and the keyboard is less comfortable to use than your laptop's. But it still does those functions (and more) well enough that you'd rather carry one device than half a dozen. The Unix philosophy[4] has its place, but shell scripts and web applications aren't the same. Visiting five different websites to accomplish one task isn't a feature.

Communication

As a program manager, your most important role is communication. The three broad categories of communication tools you'll need are: synchronous, asynchronous, and publishing. Unless the community is starting from scratch, there will probably already be some kind of communication tools in place. Use those. Don't try to push the community onto something new. But if there's a gap, fill it in.

---

4.   https://en.wikipedia.org/wiki/Unix_philosophy

For any form of communication tool, you first need to consider trust and safety. Your community hopefully has a code of conduct that defines the boundaries of acceptable behavior, but not everyone will follow that. And while your project needs the ability to enforce its rules, individuals still need the ability to enforce their own boundaries. Ben Balter has an excellent blog post[5] discussing key features that products should have for trust and safety. You can read his post for a detailed discussion, but in summary, consider if the tool you're picking gives users the ability to block or mute others, if it gives moderators the ability to hide or remove existing content, and if it can prevent users from posting new content. If the tool you pick allows contributors to be harassed out of your community, you've picked the wrong tool.

Most Tools Are Communication Tools

The previous paragraph doesn't only apply to the tools in the rest of this section. Most of the tools you use are, in some way, communication tools. This is particularly true of bug trackers and issue trackers, particularly since they're open to the public by their nature. Any website that allows user input will eventually receive spam, and a site that allows users to be "mentioned" or receive direct messages will become a vector for abuse. As you consider the rest of your toolbox, keep the trust and safety features in mind.

Synchronous Communication

Synchronous communication is primarily chat. Of course, synchronous is only fuzzily correct. In global projects, it's common to send a chat message knowing that the person you're talking to won't reply for hours. But generally, they're used for relatively instant conversation. Here are some things to consider for a synchronous communication platform.

- *Can users set a status?* Does the tool allow users to mark themselves away? Can they disable notifications? Everyone needs to step away sometimes, and being able to clearly communicate "away-ness" lets others know not to expect a reply. Multiple levels of status can be helpful. For example, "away" and "focusing" mean different things: the former means "I'm not here, so don't expect a reply," while the latter means "you can message me if it's urgent." But even a binary here/not here helps.

---

5. https://ben.balter.com/2020/08/31/trust-and-safety-features-to-build-into-your-product-before-someone-gets-hurt/

- *Does the system require authentication?* Asked another way, can users be anonymous? Authentication is helpful because it means you can enforce code of conduct violations by disabling someone's account. It gives other chat participants assurance that they're talking to whom they think they're talking to. On the other hand, if you're using chat for a user support mechanism, you might not want to require people to create an account.

- *Are chats public?* Open source communities generally operate in a transparent manner, with most communication taking place in public. Does the tool you're selecting permit this, or is read access hidden behind an authentication wall?

- *Does it support private, invitation-only chats?* On the other hand, some conversations need to happen in private. Can this be done securely, or can someone who guesses the channel name drop in uninvited?

- *Are chats logged?* Do you keep a persistent record of what is said in a chat? This can be helpful for later reference, although it might make some people uncomfortable. Similarly, what happens if someone joins a channel for the first time? Do they get to see the conversation that happened before they joined?

- *Does the tool support chatbots?* As you read in Text Meetings, on page 58, chatbots that can automatically record meeting minutes are a huge help. Chatbots can also provide other useful functions like looking up information about bugs or build status.

- *Can you interact with the tool via an API?* Similarly, you might want certain events to post messages or change a channel's topic. For example, a build failure might post a notification in the development channel while a successful build updates the channel's topic to include the latest build number.

- *Can users create ad hoc channels or does channel creation require an administrator?* Although multiple conversations can occur simultaneously in a single chat channel, sometimes it's nice to create a new channel for a particularly involved conversation.

- *Can users post images?* A picture can say a thousand words. While some communities insist on text-only communication, yours may want to support sending images.

- *How is the mobile experience?* For better or for worse, many of us are always online via our phones. For people who want that, what is the experience like? Is there an app for the popular platforms? Does the chat tool support simultaneous login sessions (for example, from a desktop and a mobile phone)? If a conversation happens on one device, can the user see it on the other device?

Asynchronous Communication

Of course, not everyone is around to chat all of the time. For more drawn-out discussions, you need an asynchronous communication platform. In most projects, this is one or more mailing lists, but forum software is making a comeback, in part because of the answers to some of the following questions.

- *Are messages publicly archived?* As with synchronous communication, it's often helpful to have public archives for later reference. Because asynchronous messages tend to be more developed thoughts, archives tend to be particularly helpful to people outside the project. By doing a web search, they can find the answers to questions that were discussed years ago.

- *Can users express agreement without creating a new message?* Have you ever been on a message thread where it seemed like every other reply was "+1"? If the tool supports adding reactions like plus signs or a thumb up, participants can express their support of an idea without adding a bunch of low-signal messages to the conversation.

- *To what extent can admins moderate conversations?* Moderation can take many forms. It could be that admins need to approve messages to a particular list or topic that's intended to be announcement-only. But it could also be the ability to move a tangent to a new thread so that the original stays on topic. Of course, admins sometimes need to remove messages that violate the community's code of conduct or even ban users from participating.

- *Can users cross-post?* The larger your community gets, the more likely it is you'll have multiple mailing lists or forum categories. What happens when someone needs to have a conversation between multiple groups? Do they need to subscribe to both venues to post? To see replies?

- *Can users edit messages?* If someone misspeaks or says something inaccurate, can they correct the original post or do they need to reply with a correction?

Publishing

Publishing is also a form of asynchronous communication. In this case, we're talking about communication that's more broadcast and less interactive. This could take the form of an announcement-only mailing list, a blog, the project's documentation website or wiki, or some combination of these. The content here would be status updates, decision announcements, and other long-term references.

- *Does the tool have a syndication feed?* An RSS feed remains a great way to get updates from a service. If the content isn't updated often, your audience won't be in the habit of checking for new information. A syndication feed can be an easy way to notify your community of updates.

- *Are diffs of edits visible?* Sometimes you have to edit the content. Can people compare the revisions to see exactly what changed?

- *Does the tool support comments?* If your community has feedback or questions about some content, can they participate in communication about the tool? Alternatively, you can point them to another asynchronous communication venue.

Bug Tracker

The bug tracker is perhaps your project's most important method for communicating with users. Used properly, it is a record of all known (and suspected) defects in the software. Often, it's also a record of all feature requests. This means you need to make the decision carefully. Given the historical context they contain—and the tooling that naturally develops around the bug tracker—it can be difficult to switch bug trackers once you've used one for a while.

Unfortunately, the internal- and external-facing nature of bug trackers often results in conflicting complexity requirements. The richness of options and settings that make a complex bug tracker appealing to developers (and the resulting richness of reportability that makes complex bug trackers appealing to program managers) can overwhelm casual users. Conversely, the simple bug trackers that give users a few simple fields can make it hard to do complex workflows on the inside. You have to decide for your project how much complexity is right and if some of it can be hidden from the casual user.

- *How much metadata can you record in separate fields?* This is the complexity we were just talking about. Developers benefit from having some information about the bug separated out into different fields that they can filter on. But too many fields add unnecessary complexity. Ideally, your bug tracker should support the fields identified in Bug Attributes, on page 117 at a minimum.

- *Are fields customizable?* Do you have control over what fields are visible and how they're described? Can you add custom fields that are important to your community's needs?

- *What metadata can users update?* Can the bug's reporter set information about the bug, or is that restricted to project members? Are some fields able to be changed by arbitrary users? (That sounds scary, but it can also enable your community to help correct misattributed bugs.) How about opening closed bugs?

- *Does the tracker link to your version control system?* If you type "fixes #12345" in a git commit, does the bug tracker notice?

- *Does the tracker support linking between bugs?* Two commonly used links in bug trackers are duplicates, where you mark a bug as being the same as another bug, and dependencies, where you indicate that resolving one bug depends on resolving another.

- *Can you perform bulk updates?* How can you update the version field on a dozen bugs that you've deferred to the next release? Can you do that in one bulk operation or does it have to be done bug by bug?

- *Does the tracker support multiple components?* If your project has multiple components, does the tracker support that? Can you move a bug from one component to another?

- *Can a bug have multiple assignees?* If multiple people are working on a bug, is that reflected in the bug's metadata? Or do you want bugs to only allow a single assignee on the theory that if more than one person is responsible, no one takes responsibility?

- *Does the tracker set a default assignee?* When a new bug is filed, does it immediately get assigned to someone? Using the list of unassigned bugs as a list of "here's how you can contribute" options is a helpful onboarding tool. On the other hand, if there's a default assignee and no progress has been made on a bug, you immediately know who to check in with.

- *Can users "watch" a particular bug or component?* If someone is interested in updates on a bug or wants to know when new bugs are filed against a component, can they set up notifications for that?

- *Can users mention other users or subscribe them to a bug?* Sometimes you know who can offer input on a bug. Does the tracker allow you to mention them in a way that sends notifications? Can you add them to the watch list so they'll get all future updates? Depending on the cultural norms of your project, this is either a must-have or a must-not-have.

- *Does the tracker have milestones or epics that bugs can link against?* This comes up most often in the context of release versions, but it can also be used for prerelease development tracking. If you have five features going into the next release, you might want to track bugs by the feature they're associated with.

- *Does the tracker provide reporting?* Being able to quickly produce some numerical stats about your bugs helps you communicate to stakeholders. How many bugs are currently open? What's the breakdown by severity? Which features are still incomplete at the beginning of the feature freeze?

- *Does the tracker allow private bugs or comments?* Public bug information is a good thing. It allows users to see what others have reported and contribute with their own results. But your community may have to deal with the occasional embargoed security fixes. Or users may post logs or core dumps that contain sensitive information. In those cases, you want to be able to restrict who can access a particular bug.

Ticket Tracker

Unlike bugs, which are defects in your software, tickets are work requests of your community. The two aren't always obviously distinct, and you can generally shoehorn tickets into a bug tracker, so many communities will combine them. For our purposes, we'll consider them as separate tools. You may find that the logical separation between the two is worth having multiple tools.

- *Can selected users vote?* One common use of ticket trackers is to submit a proposal to a group for voting. Voters can record their position by leaving a "+1" or "-1" comment, but if the tool has a native voting mechanism, that makes it easier to track the outcome. Give the tool bonus points if it can restrict voting to a defined group when appropriate.

- *Does the tool support setting due dates?* Setting a due date on a task is a good way to motivate people to get it done. The due date doesn't have to be for completing the task; you can set a date for when the next update is due. This helps when building meeting agendas.

- *Does the tool support adding labels?* Tagging a ticket with the "meeting" label is an excellent way to put something on the agenda for the next meeting. Labels are also useful for categorizing tickets. For example, if someone is asking for money to set up a booth at a conference, you might tag it with "budget" and "events."

- *Can tickets be linked to other tickets?* As with bugs, you'll sometimes want to indicate that a ticket is blocked until another ticket is handled.

- *Do tickets have a state?* Some tickets are simple tasks that are either done or not done. Others require work that takes some time. If the ticket tracker allows tickets to be in different states, it's easier for you to track what's going on. If the tracker has kanban board functionality, that's sufficient. Labels will work in a pinch, but you may end up with ambiguous combinations. What does it mean, for example, if a ticket has both "in progress" and "blocked" labels?

- *Are different closed types supported?* As with bugs, knowing something is closed isn't always sufficient. If the tracker is used for proposals, you may want to be able to easily distinguish between tickets closed because they were approved versus tickets closed because they were rejected. Labels can be used here, too, but they're not ideal.

- *Does the tracker support private tickets?* Most open source work happens in the public view, but occasionally you need to handle sensitive information. This can include votes on whether to grant someone commit access or addressing code of conduct violations. If the ticket tracker supports private tickets, you can handle sensitive requests alongside the routine public work.

Kanban Board

Kanban, if you're not familiar with it, is a system of tracking work. Tasks are put on cards. When they're ready, a member of the team pulls a card from the "to do" column and moves it to the "doing" column. When it's done, they move it to the "done" column. Kanban doesn't define a pace of work, team members move cards when they're ready. The visibility of a board allows everyone to quickly see the state of tasks. Although it was designed for teams working in manufacturing, you'll find it helps track work for yourself, too.

Ideally, your kanban board will be a feature of your ticket tracker. This way you can see your work in both list and board form. But let's discuss kanban boards on their own because they're incredibly useful at tracking the state of work you have in flight. And as a program manager, you'll have a lot of work to keep track of. For examples of kanban in practice, see *Real-World Kanban [Ska15]* by Mattias Skarin.

- *Are the columns customizable?* Many kanban tools start out with three basic columns: "to do," "doing," and "done." But you might want to add additional columns like "waiting for feedback." My writing board that I use for blog posts and submitted articles has columns "ideas," "researching," "writing," "editing," "queued," and "published."

- *Can columns have a work-in-progress limit?* One of the features of the kanban process is keeping work in progress to a manageable limit. If you have 10 things you're working on simultaneously, you're probably making little progress on any of them. Setting a work-in-progress limit on your columns forces you to get work done before moving on to the next thing. If something is blocked, you can move it out of the doing column until it gets unblocked.

- *Does the tool support setting due dates?* As with tickets, setting a due date on a kanban card is a good way to remind yourself of when something is due. Give the tool bonus points if the due dates can be represented in a calendar view.

- *Can you add subtasks or use epics?* In basic form, kanban cards represent single, independent tasks. In practice, tasks are often related. For example, to produce a release announcement, you might have tasks for writing the blog post and designing a cover image. These tasks can be done independently, but they're ultimately a part of the release announcement task, which isn't done until all subtasks are done. Being able to cleanly represent these relationships helps.

- *Can custom labels be applied to cards?* As with tickets, giving a label to describe the type of task helps provide visual clues and lets you filter on the type of work. If you've been doing a lot of a particular kind of work lately, you might pick something with a different label when you go to look at what to work on next.

Schedule Builder

You could present your schedule in a simple table in a text or HTML file, but that makes changes challenging. If you change one date, you want the related dates to change as well. Many tools that allow you to build schedules also include many features you won't use: personnel allocation, budgeting, and so on. They're largely designed with corporate projects in mind, but you can safely ignore the extra features. For small projects with simple schedules, a spreadsheet may work well enough. They can do date math for you. For larger or more complicated schedules, there are other considerations.

- *Can you set multiple scenarios?* You know as soon as you make a schedule that it's going to be wrong. You don't know *how* it will be wrong, but you can often think of a few likely scenarios. If the tool allows you to create an alternate scenario where the beta release is two weeks late, for example, this can make the results of decisions easier to understand.

- *Does the schedule fit when being stored in a version control system?* Much of an open source project lives in a version control system, so it's nice if the schedule source does as well. This allows you to create several alternate versions in different branches when proposing changes. It also gives the community the opportunity to make changes directly by submitting a patch. Of course, "can be stored in version control" and "are easy for humans to work with" don't entirely overlap. Large XML files, which are used by some tools, can be stored in a version control system but are painful for humans to use directly.

- *Can schedules be linked to each other?* Sometimes elements on one release's schedule are linked to another's. For example, Fedora Linux N reaches end of life four weeks after Fedora Linux N+2's release. If your tool can directly link between releases, that saves you some manual updates.

- *Can teams submit updates on their tasks?* The schedule only tells you what *should be*, not what *is*. If the tool allows teams to indicate how close they are to the schedule, that gives you additional insight into the current status. For example, if the documentation team has two weeks on the schedule to write release notes and they're done 10 days in, it'd be nice if they could indicate that. Similarly, if at the 10-day mark, they're only 10% done, that's helpful information for you to know as well.

- *Does the tool build filtered views of the schedule?* A large community's release schedule can have a hundred or more tasks. That makes it difficult for contributors to see the areas they care about. Ideally, you'd want your tool to be able to produce different renderings of the schedule broken out by a team or other logical grouping. This way the website team can see just their tasks, the infrastructure team can see just their tasks, and so on.

- *Does the tool support graphical views of the schedule?* Listings and tables are one thing, but sometimes it helps to look at a picture. If your tool can produce a calendar view (or generate an ICS file that people can import to their calendars), that helps give a better sense of timing. Gantt charts (see Gantt Chart, on page 22) provide an easy-to-follow representation of both time and dependencies.

Retrospective

You now have the knowledge to pick the tools for your toolbox. This appendix doesn't include a complete set of everything needed to make an open source project go. Some tools, such as a git repo, are more project-wide considerations and less the domain of the program manager. As you go, you'll pick up other tools that you find valuable: scripting languages, data analysis tools, and so on. For now, though, you have a good start.

Bibliography

[Bro95]   Frederick P. Brooks Jr. *The Mythical Man-Month: Essays on Software Engineering*. Addison-Wesley, Boston, MA, Anniversary, 1995.

[Fog17]   Karl Fogel. *Producing Open Source Software: How to Run a Successful Free Software Project*. O'Reilly & Associates, Inc., Sebastopol, CA, Second, 2017.

[Lim06]   Thomas A. Limoncelli. *Time Management For System Administrators*. O'Reilly & Associates, Inc., Sebastopol, CA, 2006.

[Rot07]   Johanna Rothman. *Manage It!*. The Pragmatic Bookshelf, Raleigh, NC, 2007.

[Ska15]   Mattias Skarin. *Real-World Kanban*. The Pragmatic Bookshelf, Raleigh, NC, 2015.

Index

Thank you!

We hope you enjoyed this book and that you're already thinking about what you want to learn next. To help make that decision easier, we're offering you this gift.

Head on over to https://pragprog.com right now, and use the coupon code BUYANOTHER2022 to save 30% on your next ebook. Offer is void where prohibited or restricted. This offer does not apply to any edition of the *The Pragmatic Programmer* ebook.

And if you'd like to share your own expertise with the world, why not propose a writing idea to us? After all, many of our best authors started off as our readers, just like you. With a 50% royalty, world-class editorial services, and a name you trust, there's nothing to lose. Visit https://pragprog.com/become-an-author/ today to learn more and to get started.

We thank you for your continued support, and we hope to hear from you again soon!

The Pragmatic Bookshelf

Effective Remote Work

The office isn't as essential as it used to be. Flexible working hours and distributed teams are replacing decades of on-site, open-plan office culture. Wherever you work from nowadays, your colleagues are likely to be somewhere else. No more whiteboards. No more water coolers. And certainly no Ping-Pong. So how can you organize yourself, ship software, communicate, and be impactful as part of a globally distributed workforce? We'll show you how. It's time to adopt a brand new mindset. Remote working is here to stay. Come and join us.

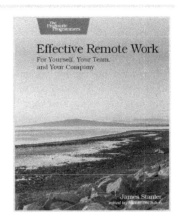

James Stanier
(348 pages) ISBN: 9781680509229. $47.95
https://pragprog.com/book/jsrw

Build Talking Apps for Alexa

Voice recognition is here at last. Alexa and other voice assistants have now become widespread and mainstream. Is your app ready for voice interaction? Learn how to develop your own voice applications for Amazon Alexa. Start with techniques for building conversational user interfaces and dialog management. Integrate with existing applications and visual interfaces to complement voice-first applications. The future of human-computer interaction is voice, and we'll help you get ready for it.

Craig Walls
(388 pages) ISBN: 9781680507256. $47.95
https://pragprog.com/book/cwalexa

Help Your Boss Help You

Develop more productive habits in dealing with your manager. As a professional in the business world, you care about doing your job the right way. The quality of your work matters to you, both as a professional and as a person. The company you work for cares about making money and your boss is evaluated on that basis. Sometimes those goals overlap, but the different priorities mean conflict is inevitable. Take concrete steps to build a relationship with your manager that helps both sides succeed.

Ken Kousen
(160 pages) ISBN: 9781680508222. $26.95
https://pragprog.com/book/kkmanage

Become an Effective Software Engineering Manager

Software startups make global headlines every day. As technology companies succeed and grow, so do their engineering departments. In your career, you'll may suddenly get the opportunity to lead teams: to become a manager. But this is often uncharted territory. How do you decide whether this career move is right for you? And if you do, what do you need to learn to succeed? Where do you start? How do you know that you're doing it right? What does "it" even mean? And isn't management a dirty word? This book will share the secrets you need to know to manage engineers successfully.

James Stanier
(396 pages) ISBN: 9781680507249. $45.95
https://pragprog.com/book/jsengman

Rust Brain Teasers

The Rust programming language is consistent and does its best to avoid surprising the programmer. Like all languages, though, Rust still has its quirks. But these quirks present a teaching opportunity. In this book, you'll work through a series of brain teasers that will challenge your understanding of Rust. By understanding the gaps in your knowledge, you can become better at what you do and avoid mistakes. Many of the teasers in this book come from the author's own experience creating software. Others derive from commonly asked questions in the Rust community. Regardless of their origin, these brain teasers are fun, and let's face it: who doesn't love a good puzzle, right?

Herbert Wolverson
(138 pages) ISBN: 9781680509175. $18.95
https://pragprog.com/book/hwrustbrain

Powerful Command-Line Applications in Go

Write your own fast, reliable, and cross-platform command-line tools with the Go programming language. Go might be the fastest—and perhaps the most fun—way to automate tasks, analyze data, parse logs, talk to network services, or address other systems requirements. Create all kinds of command-line tools that work with files, connect to services, and manage external processes, all while using tests and benchmarks to ensure your programs are fast and correct.

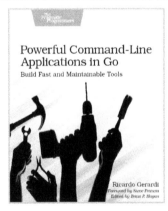

Ricardo Gerardi
(508 pages) ISBN: 9781680506969. $45.95
https://pragprog.com/book/rggo

Kotlin and Android Development featuring Jetpack

Start building native Android apps the modern way in Kotlin with Jetpack's expansive set of tools, libraries, and best practices. Learn how to create efficient, resilient views with Fragments and share data between the views with ViewModels. Use Room to persist valuable data quickly, and avoid NullPointerExceptions and Java's verbose expressions with Kotlin. You can even handle asynchronous web service calls elegantly with Kotlin coroutines. Achieve all of this and much more while building two full-featured apps, following detailed, step-by-step instructions.

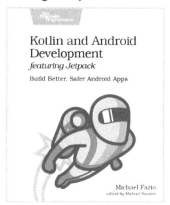

Michael Fazio
(444 pages) ISBN: 9781680508154. $49.95
https://pragprog.com/book/mfjetpack

Learn to Program, Third Edition

It's easier to learn how to program a computer than it has ever been before. Now everyone can learn to write programs for themselves—no previous experience is necessary. Chris Pine takes a thorough, but lighthearted approach that teaches you the fundamentals of computer programming, with a minimum of fuss or bother. Whether you are interested in a new hobby or a new career, this book is your doorway into the world of programming.

Chris Pine
(230 pages) ISBN: 9781680508178. $45.95
https://pragprog.com/book/ltp3

Portable Python Projects

Discover easy ways to control your home with the powerful new Raspberry Pi hardware. Program short Python scripts that will detect changes in your home and react with the instructions you code. Use new add-on accessories to monitor a variety of measurements, from light intensity and temperature to motion detection and water leakage. Expand the base projects with your own custom additions to perfectly match your own home setup. Most projects in the book can be completed in under an hour, giving you more time to enjoy and tweak your autonomous creations. No breadboard or electronics knowledge required!

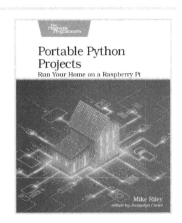

Mike Riley
(180 pages) ISBN: 9781680508598. $45.95
https://pragprog.com/book/mrpython

Modern CSS with Tailwind, Second Edition

Tailwind CSS is an exciting new CSS framework that allows you to design your site by composing simple utility classes to create complex effects. With Tailwind, you can style your text, move your items on the page, design complex page layouts, and adapt your design for devices from a phone to a wide-screen monitor. With this book, you'll learn how to use the Tailwind for its flexibility and its consistency, from the smallest detail of your typography to the entire design of your site.

Noel Rappin
(102 pages) ISBN: 9781680509403. $29.95
https://pragprog.com/book/tailwind2

The Pragmatic Bookshelf

The Pragmatic Bookshelf features books written by professional developers for professional developers. The titles continue the well-known Pragmatic Programmer style and continue to garner awards and rave reviews. As development gets more and more difficult, the Pragmatic Programmers will be there with more titles and products to help you stay on top of your game.

Visit Us Online

This Book's Home Page
https://pragprog.com/book/bcosp
Source code from this book, errata, and other resources. Come give us feedback, too!

Keep Up to Date
https://pragprog.com
Join our announcement mailing list (low volume) or follow us on twitter @pragprog for new titles, sales, coupons, hot tips, and more.

New and Noteworthy
https://pragprog.com/news
Check out the latest pragmatic developments, new titles and other offerings.

Save on the ebook

Save on the ebook versions of this title. Owning the paper version of this book entitles you to purchase the electronic versions at a terrific discount.

PDFs are great for carrying around on your laptop—they are hyperlinked, have color, and are fully searchable. Most titles are also available for the iPhone and iPod touch, Amazon Kindle, and other popular e-book readers.

Send a copy of your receipt to support@pragprog.com and we'll provide you with a discount coupon.

Contact Us

Online Orders:	*https://pragprog.com/catalog*
Customer Service:	*support@pragprog.com*
International Rights:	*translations@pragprog.com*
Academic Use:	*academic@pragprog.com*
Write for Us:	*http://write-for-us.pragprog.com*
Or Call:	+1 800-699-7764

9 781680 509243